# MARKET LEADER

## Business Grammar and Usage

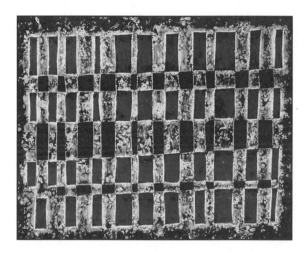

## BUSINESS ENGLISH

Peter Strutt

Longman

**FINANCIAL TIMES**
World business newspaper.

**Pearson Education Limited**
Edinburgh Gate
Harlow
Essex CM20 2JE
England
and Associated Companies throughout the World

First published 2000
Eighth impression 2004

ISBN 0 582 365759

Set in 10/12.5pt Apolline, 10.5/12.5pt MetaPlus

Printed in Malaysia

www.market-leader.net

### Acknowledgements

We are grateful to the following for permission to reproduce copyright material:
Guardian News Service for an extract from the article 'From cars to cans of beer' by N.O.Byrne in *THE GUARDIAN* 24.2.99; Societe des Produits Nestle S.A., owner of the trademarks NESCAFE, NESTLE, NESTEA, BUITONI, MAGGIE, FRISKIES, for an extract from *Nestle Management Report* 1999; United States Geological Survey for an adapted extract from *U.S. GEOLOGICAL SURVEY*.

We have been unable to trace the copyright holder of the articles 'I understand what makes a chick tick' in *BUSINESS AGE* August 1998, 'The Boy from Nowhere' in *BUSINESS AGE* March 1999 or material taken from the *Kodak* website www.kodak.com and would appreciate any information which would enable us to do so.

### Illustration acknowledgements

Nick Baker for 69, 95, 141, 142, 155; Jeremy Banx for 24, 53, 55, 56, 62, 122, 125, 126, ; Roger Beale for 10, 115, 150; Dave Bowyer for 50, 120, 129 (both), 204; Celia Hart for 143; Katherine Walker for 11, 29, 45, 117, 161, 167, 174, 176, 177;

### Photo acknowledgements

We are grateful to the following for permission to reproduce copyright photographs:
Camera Press for 23 right, 89 left and 89 right; Euro Business Magazine/Graham Fudger for 147; Hulton Getty for 14; Popperfoto for 21; Quadrant Picture Library for 89 middle; Rex Features for 59 and Universal Pictorial Press and Agency for 23 middle and 23 right.

The cover photograph has been kindly supplied by Photonica.

Project Managed by Chris Hartley

# Contents

# Present tenses

## Present simple (1)

**Form**

I / you / we / they **work.**
He / she / it **works.**

I / you / we / they **do** not **work.**
He / she / it **does** not **work.**

**Do** I / you / we / they **work?**
**Does** he / she / it **work?**

**Uses**

**1** Presenting factual information, e.g. about company activities

Our company **employs** over 100,000 people, **operates** in many overseas markets, and **offers** a wide-range of hi-tech products for the 21st century.

**2** Actions and situations which are generally true

Imperial Tobacco **belongs to** the Hanson group.
High taxation **discourages** investment.
We **sell** our products into many markets.
A good brand **guarantees** a certain level of quality to customers.
British wines usually **have** a sweet taste.
Competition **brings out** the best in products and the worst in people.

**3** Verbs used only in the present simple

There are a number of verbs which are almost always used in the present simple and not with -*ing*. These verbs usually refer to:

**mental states**: believe, doubt, forget, imagine, know, realise, recognise, regret, remember, suppose, think, understand
**likes and dislikes:** admire, dislike, hate, like, love, want, wish
**possession:** belong to, contain, have, include, own, possess
**appearance:** appear, look like, resemble, seem
**being:** be, consist of, depend, exist
**perception:** hear, see, smell, taste

**4** Saying how often you or other people do things

We usually use the present simple with frequency adverbs:

I *never* **smoke** at work.
He **plays** golf *every Sunday morning.*
I *often* **take** files home at the weekend.
When she **gets** to the office she *always* **checks** her e-mail first.

## Practice

**A Mission statements**

A mission statement talks in general terms about a company's overall policies and objectives. Read the two mission statements below and use the verbs to complete them, paying attention to the verb endings. The first one has been done for you in both cases.

> ~~admit~~  introduce  lead  welcome  mean
> work  depend  improve  stay  come  spend

Restless? Yes. Dissatisfied? True. We cheerfully ......._admit_...... it. We always ..................[1] change and continuous improvement. Today consumers .............[2] more than $25 billion a year on our products. We ..................[3] – or ..................[4] a very close second – in all our business segments, which ..................[5] that vigorous growth ..................[6] on our own imagination, commitment and skill. So we regularly ..................[7] new products, ..................[8] distribution channels and..................[9] round the clock to be more efficient. Most of all, we ..................[10] absolutely, and unequivocally, 100% geared towards the customer, who's definitely No. 1 in our book!

> ~~believe~~  strive  cultivate  deliver  enable  help
> give  endeavour  acknowledge  foster

Eastman Kodak Company ......._believes_..... that a diverse group of highly skilled people, in an organisational culture which ..................[11] them to apply their collective talents to shared objectives, ..................[12] the greatest value to customers and shareowners alike. The company and its employees ..................[13] to support an inclusive Kodak culture that ..................[14] unique thinking in the context of teamwork and common business goals. Kodak ..................[15] to provide a flexible, supportive work environment that ..................[16] employees as partners in the business and community. To this end, it ..................[17] employees access to a multitude of work/life resources and..................[18] programs that ..................[19] individuals balance their commitment to meeting business needs with their personal, family, and community responsibilities.

**B General truths**

Complete these sayings appropriately, using these verbs.

> buy  believe  believe  tend  promise  say  put  mean  talk

1 'Every time we .................. a foreign car we .................. someone else out of work.'
   (Woodrow Wyatt)

2 'Money .................. they .................. ; all it ever said to me was "Goodbye".'
   (Cary Grant)

3 'Democracy .................. government by discussion but it is only effective if you can stop people talking.' (Clement Attlee, British Prime Minister)

4 'Politicians are the same all over. They .................. to build a bridge even where there's no river.'
   (Khrushchev)

5 'In a hierarchy every employee .................. to rise to his level of incompetence.' (L. J. Peter)

6 'Not all Germans .................. in God, but they .................. in the Bundesbank.'
   (Jacques Delors)

## Present simple (2)

**5** Asking for and giving directions and instructions

'How do I **get** to your office?'

'You **turn** left after the station, **cross** the bridge and it's the second building on your right.'

**Place** the CD in the drive and **click** on the icon.

**6** Talking about timetables and scheduled events

The bus **leaves** at 8.35 tomorrow morning.

The exhibition **opens** on 25 January.

The legislation **comes** into force on 1 January.

These are seen as fixed and the speaker is unlikely to be able to influence them.

Future 2.5 page 30

**7** Providing a summary or abstract at the beginning of a report

The first section of this report **provides** introductory comments, **focuses** on important new developments and **highlights** some of our operations outside the United States. The second section **analyses** the results for the group as a whole. The final two sections **address** our consolidated cash flows and financial condition. The report **concludes** by pointing out the need for further investment if the group is to continue its expansion policy.

**8** Newspaper headlines

The use of the present simple creates a sense of dramatic impact.

Unilever sells coffee operations

**Russia doubles tea import duties**

**MARKETS TUMBLE AS INVESTORS TAKE PROFITS**

PepsiCo link with Suntory

Shortages force up food prices

BANK REGULATOR BLOCKS MERGER

**9** Doing by saying

We use the present simple with certain verbs which say what their function is. When we say them we 'perform' the action. For example, saying 'I **promise** to meet you at the airport' is making a promise. Other examples include:

I **resign**!                          I **apologise**.

I **declare** this meeting open.        I **demand** to see the manager.

I **admit** I was wrong.                I **advise** you to look again at our proposal.

**Practice**

## A A travel booking

Read the following dialogue about travel arrangements. Make any necessary changes to the verbs in brackets.

**Traveller** Hello, I ..................[1] (need) to go to London next Friday and come back on the same day. I've a meeting which ..................[2] (start) at 11 o'clock.

**Agent** .................. you ..................[3] (want) to fly or take the train?

**Traveller** That ..................[4] (depend) on the price. How much .................. it ..................[5] (cost)?

**Agent** The train ..................[6] (be) cheaper and ..................[7] (get) you right into the centre of London. It ..................[8] (take) just three hours.

**Traveller** OK, that's fine. What about times?

**Agent** Well, the Eurostar ..................[9] (leave) Paris at 7.19 and ..................[10] (arrive) in London at 10.13 local time.

**Traveller** What time .................. I ..................[11] (have to) check in?

**Agent** Not later than 20 minutes before departure.

**Traveller** OK, How .................. I ..................[12] (make) a reservation?

## B A summary of a report

Complete the introduction to this report, using these verbs.

| highlight   recommend   focus   call for   provide |
|---|

This report ..................[1] on the employment of women and children in a number of emerging nations. In particular, it ..................[2] the conditions endured by thousands of workers in places where child labour, poverty wages and health risks are endemic. Each chapter ..................[3] an analysis of the situation on a country-by-country basis.

The report ..................[4] that retailers should lay down tough rules to make sure overseas suppliers pay sufficient wages to meet basic needs. It also..................[5] companies to draw up a code of conduct and employ inspectors to make manufacturers keep it.

## C Headlines

Match the beginning and ends of the headlines.

1 FORD SEEKS TO CUT
2 BOURSES SLIP
3 SÃO PAULO DEBT CRISIS
4 CHINA RENEWS ATTACK
5 PESSIMISTS FORESEE
6 UNDERWATER VENTURE NEEDS

a) SENDS OUT SHOCK WAVES
b) DEATH OF EMPLOYMENT
c) ON US TECHNOLOGY REPORT
d) BACKING TO STAY AFLOAT
e) AS DOLLAR FALLS AGAINST YEN
f) 1bn IN COSTS

## Present progressive (1)

**Form**

I **am working**.
You / we / they **are working**.
He / she / it **is working**.

I **am** not **working**.
You / we / they **are** not **working**.
He / she / it **is** not **working**.

**Am** I **working?**
**Are** you / we / they **working**?
**Is** he / she / it **working**?

**Uses**

**1** Talking about an event in progress at the moment of speaking

'What **are** you **doing**?' '**I'm trying** to find a file.'
I'm afraid Mr Bansall can't see you right now. He**'s interviewing** someone.

We also often use the progressive with verbs of movement when the action has just started:

**I'm leaving**. Can you tell Rosemary I'll see her tomorrow?
'Can I speak to John?' 'Sorry, he's out. No, hold on, he**'s** just **coming** down the corridor.'

**2** Describing current situations and ongoing projects

The time reference is at and around 'now', before and after the situations referred to. But the situation may not be in progress literally at the exact moment of speaking.

We**'re waiting** for permission to go ahead with the project.
Big Japanese companies **are thinking** again about uniform pay systems.
My boss **is dealing** with your enquiry but you won't get a rapid answer.

From the *Financial Times*

**3** Describing temporary situations

When the present progressive is used in this way, the situation described will not last permanently.

They**'re staying** at the Crillon Hotel until the end of the week.
He**'s working** in Libya on a fixed-term contract.
They **are offering** a 20% discount for the duration of the trade fair.

## Practice

### A Events in progress

Look at the pictures and decide what is happening in each one.

### B News in brief

Read these extracts about projects that various companies are currently involved in.
Match the extracts in column A with those in column B.

**A**

1 Ford is aiming to corner 10% of car sales in the Asia-Pacific region within the next 10 years.

2 IBM in Europe chooses schools with the technology to teach collaboration, writes Della Bradshaw.

3 Showa Shell Sekiyu and Cosmo Oil are stepping up plans to cut costs and improve cash flow.

4 The New Zealand government has decided to sell the country's second-biggest electricity generator.

5 Sales of DVD video should take off in Europe next year when nearly 500,000 players will be sold, according to a new study.

**B**

a) The chief reforms are the elimination of 900 jobs and the reduction of sales, general and administrative expenses.

b) The firm is opting for external management training in a big way and is using its purchasing power to push the business schools involved into adopting the very latest technology to deliver their courses.

c) After a slow start, the compact disc version of the video cassette is now selling well in North America.

d) It currently has about 1% of the region's market but hopes to significantly expand its operations in China, Japan, Thailand and India.

e) It is seeking commercial advisers for the sale of Contact Energy, which produces 27% of the country's energy supply.

### C Temporary situations

Complete these sentences appropriately.

1 There are no trains this week because of the strike so ...
2 Her boss is off sick at the moment so ...
3 We've got builders in our house so ...
4 There are rumours of a devaluation so ...

## Present progressive (2)

### 4 Changing, developing situations

We use the present progressive to describe changes which have not yet finished:

The number of people using the Internet **is growing**.
The Amazon rainforest **is disappearing** at an alarming rate.
Consumers in the industrialised world **are becoming** increasingly concerned with healthy living.

### 5 Personal arrangements and plans

We use the present progressive to refer to future time when talking about arrangements and fixed plans made before the time of speaking. We often use a time expression unless we are sure that the other person knows we are talking about the future:

I**'m seeing** Mr Poorhassan next weekend.
I**'m taking** the client to the best restaurant in town.
She's got a new job so she**'s leaving** the firm in October.

We also use the present progressive with verbs of movement to talk about actions which are just beginning:

It's 1 o'clock. I**'m going** to the canteen for lunch. **Are** you **coming**?

### 6 Talking about repeated actions

His daughter **is taking** driving lessons.
His wife **is** always **telling** him not to work so hard.
We **are** constantly **monitoring** our products for quality.

If we describe repeated situations using the present progressive with *always*, the situation is often unplanned. Compare:

I always **meet** Marilyn in the car park. (planned in advance)
I**'m** always **meeting** Marilyn in the car park. (by chance)

**Practice**

**A Changes**

Write about the changes the government of your country is currently making in the following sectors, as in the example.

Example:

business and finance   *The government is setting up new enterprise schemes.*

1 the environment ...................................................................

2 taxation ............................................................................

3 the law ............................................................................

4 transportation ...................................................................

5 education .........................................................................

6 health .............................................................................

**B Arrangements**

Complete this dialogue appropriately, using verbs in the present progressive.

**A** Are you free next Wednesday?

**B** No, sorry. I'm afraid I .......................................................[1]

**A** Well, I can't make it on Thursday so what about Friday?

**B** In the morning I .......................................................[2] but in the afternoon I
.......................................................[3] anything special.

**A** Fine, that's OK by me.

**C Present simple or present progressive?**

Which of these ideas do you associate with the present simple (PS) and which with the present progressive (PP)?

1 regular activities ............

2 temporary situations ............

3 fixed timetables ............

4 giving instructions ............

5 an event in progress ............

6 permanent and factual situations ............

7 a present arrangement for the future ............

8 mental states ............

9 trends and changing situations ............

10 doing by saying ............

Study these sentences and decide which example corresponds to each of 1–10 above.

**a)** I'm replacing Bill because he's off sick.

**b)** The scheduled flight leaves next Monday at 8.15 from JFK.

**c)** The technician is mending the photocopier so you can't use it right now.

**d)** I'm seeing Bill Sykes tomorrow afternoon, I've got it in my diary.

**e)** The conference room measures 164 square metres.

**f)** I admit there has been a mistake.

**g)** I understand they have gone bankrupt.

**h)** Enter PIN number, select menu, choose language, press OK.

**i)** With the Internet the world is getting smaller.

**j)** We have a planning meeting once a month.

# UNIT 2 Past tenses

## Past simple

**Form**

I / you / he / she / it / we / they **worked**.
I / you / he / she / it / we / they **did** not **work**.
**Did** I / you / he / she / it / we / they **work**?

I / he / she / it **was** late.
You / we / they **were** late.
**Was** I / he / she / it late?
**Were** you / we / they late?

**Uses**

**1 Talking about completed actions that happened in the past**

Alexander Graham Bell **invented** the telephone.
'**Did** you read the contract?' 'Yes, and I **sent** it back to the legal department.'

**2 Referring to a definite moment or period in the past**

I **met** the president *yesterday*.
I **spoke** to them *an hour ago*.
Ted Turner **launched** CNN *in 1980*.
The standard of living in Europe **went up** *during the 1960s*.
Did you **discuss** the problem *at last week's meeting*?

**3 Describing something, e.g. the history of a company**

When George Eastman **introduced** the first Kodak camera in 1888, he **wanted** to supply the tools of photography at the lowest possible price to the greatest number of people. The rapid growth of his business **made** large-scale production a necessity. The creation of ingenious tools and processes for manufacturing film **enabled** the Eastman company to turn out high-quality merchandise at prices that **put** them within the reach of the general public.

**4 In reports, e.g. a company's annual report**

We use the past simple in annual reports when they refer back to the previous year's trading:

Last year **was** a tough year for our group. On the one hand, we **earned** more than a billion dollars, we **generated** record cash flow and many of our businesses **posted** big gains in sales, profit and market share. On the other hand, our total earnings **declined**, our overseas subsidiaries **experienced** major problems and our US production facilities **underperformed**.

## Practice

### A Important firsts

What made these people famous? Write true sentences, and change the form of the verb.

Example: *John Logie Baird gave the first public demonstration of television in 1926.*

| | | | |
|---|---|---|---|
| **1** | John Logie Baird | invent | the first flight in 1903. |
| **2** | The Wright brothers | discover | radium in 1902. |
| **3** | Neil Armstrong | make | the first commercial sewing machine in 1851. |
| **4** | Pierre and Marie Curie | patent | the first public demonstration of television in 1926. |
| **5** | Gutenberg | give | the printing press in 1434. |
| **6** | Isaac Singer | land | on the surface of the moon in 1969. |

### B The Bell story

Complete each paragraph, using the verbs in the boxes.

> have   say   begin   introduce   open

In 1985 Simon Bell ..................[1] his computer business at the University of Southampton. In 1987 his company ..................[2] the Z5000 machine which the magazine *PC Journal* ..................[3] 'may become the next industry benchmark'. The following year he ..................[4] an office in the United States and soon ..................[5] offices in 28 countries.

> amount   decide   employ   run   go

In 1989, Bell ..................[6] public. By now the firm ..................[7] 750 people and sales ..................[8] to over $159 million. Then two years later employees ..................[9] to celebrate 1 April by hanging a giant inflatable banana outside company headquarters, the first of many publicity stunts. On another occasion the CEO ..................[10] the London marathon.

> set up   launch   total   offer

In 1992 Bell ..................[11] free installation of applications software as a standard option and in 1993 ..................[12] the low-priced Explorer PCs, one of the most highly praised systems in the industry. In 1996 Bell ..................[13] an Internet computer store, through its website www.bell.com. Last year sales ..................[14] more than $10 million a day.

### C An annual report

Complete the extract choosing from these verbs. There are more verbs than necessary.

> delay   choose   improve   give   make   stabilise   hinder

Last year the international situation in the hydrocarbons industry ..................[1] to some extent. However, the volatile foreign exchange rates ..................[2] currency management more difficult and relatively weak demand ..................[3] expansion projects. We therefore ..................[4] to focus our efforts on specific opportunities where our know-how ..................[5] us a technical advantage over particularly aggressive competition. As a result we propose doubling our dividend.

## Past progressive

**Form**  I **was working**.
You / we / they **were working**.
He / she / it **was working**.

I **was** not **working**.
You / we / they **were** not **working**.
He / she / it **was** not **working**.

**Was** I **working**?
**Were** you / we / they **working**?
**Was** he / she / it **working**?

**Uses**  **1**  Emphasising the duration or continuity of a past event

He **was working** on the report all day long.
During the 1990s computer scientists **were trying** to deal with the millennium bug.

**2**  Describing a background event

We use the past progressive to describe an event which was in progress when it was interrupted by another one. The second, shorter event, is in the past simple:

I **was** just **leaving** the office when he **arrived**.
We **were talking** about safety procedures when the fire alarm **went off**.

**3**  For repeated events

He **was visiting** clients all last week and didn't come into the office. (a number of different clients)
Last month we **were having** a lot of problems with the production line. (a number of different problems)

However, the past progressive is *not* normally used for the same action which is repeated, or for habitual past actions:

The production line **stopped** five times yesterday. (NOT *was stopping)
When I was at business school we often **worked** on case studies. (NOT *were working on)

**4**  Making polite requests

I **was wondering** if you could give me a lift downtown.

There is no idea of past time here. The past verb form is a polite formula and makes the request less direct.

**5**  For events planned in the past which did not take place

I **was planning** to visit the exhibition but I went to the football match instead.
She **was going** to phone them yesterday but didn't have the time.

## Practice

**A The reasons why**

Use the words in the box to give explanations for the following events.
The first has been done for you.

| | |
|---|---|
| ~~funds~~ | plummet |
| the president | suffer |
| the fire bell | ~~run out~~ |
| my work | complain |
| their value | ring |
| customers | speak |

1 We scrapped the project because ......... *funds were running out.* ...............................

2 They evacuated the building because ..................................................................

3 He sold his shares quickly because ....................................................................

4 He didn't wish to interrupt because ...................................................................

5 I cut down on drinking because .........................................................................

6 We were forced to withdraw the model because ...................................................

**B Steve Jobs**

Read the following passage and choose where to insert these sentences.

**a)** Magazines such as *Fortune* and *Business Week* were all mocking him.

**b)** But it is true that Jobs was still losing money. In the early 1990s he was going bankrupt at an alarming rate.

**c)** Pixar Animation Inc. was also bleeding cash fast.

**d)** His two businesses, Next (a computer firm) and Pixar (a computer animation company), were rapidly going bankrupt.

> Entrepreneurs can go through long periods of bad luck and fall on hard times. Steve Jobs, the founder of Apple, is one of these people. Since enjoying tremendous success in the 1980s he spent 11 years of humiliating failure.
>
> After he was sacked by Apple, he lost millions of dollars by selling his shares at the wrong time. ..................[1]. Next had spent $180 million of its shareholders' money and had nothing to show for it. ..................[2].
>
> For five years, the criticism from the business press was universal and deafening. ..................[3]. Then a writer called Randall Stross published a book called Steve Jobs and the Next Big Thing which accused him, among other things, of fostering false optimism on successes that didn't exist and having no financial know-how. It was a humiliating attack. ..................[4]. By 1995 he had lost $200m out of a fortune of $300m.
>
> Now all that is behind him. Pixar now makes animated movies in partnership with Disney. Toy Story was the third-highest earning animation of all time and the launch of the iMac was a huge success. We haven't heard the last of Mr Jobs.

## Past perfect simple

**Form**   I / you / we / they **had worked**.  **Had** I / you / we / they **worked**?
He / she / it **had worked**.  **Had** he / she / it **worked**?

I / you / we / they **had** not **worked**.
He / she / it **had** not **worked**.

**Uses**   **1**   **Talking about events that happened before other events**

In this extract the events in bold type refer to an earlier past:

*had climbed into the dryer* = before the accident
*his employer had not given him proper training* = before the accident
*had been an unlawful killing* = before the trial
*had died* = before the trial

Paul Bennett was killed after he **had climbed** into a giant industrial tumble dryer to free a piece of cloth trapped inside. The machine started accidentally and he was spun to death at a heat of 43°C. It became evident that his employer **had not given** him proper training and a jury decided that there **had been** an 'unlawful killing' – it was satisfied beyond reasonable doubt that Mr Bennett **had died** as a result of manslaughter.

**2**   **With *I wish, If only* and *I'd rather***

We use the past perfect to talk about events that did not happen:

I wish I **had been** more interested in English at school.
If only I **had bought** those shares; they've gone up 27%.
I'd rather he**'d asked** me before taking my car.

In the negative, the sentence expresses a regret for events that did take place:

He wishes he **hadn't left** his previous job. (but he did)

**3**   **Emphasising the recent nature and/or duration of actions**

If we want to focus on continuous activity taking place in an earlier past we use the progressive form:

earlier past          past                          present

They **had been testing** the drug for years before it came onto the market.
She had to take a break because she**'d been working** far too hard.

**Practice**

**A Susan George's CV**

Read the CV and complete the sentences about Susan George using these verbs.

| develop   market   be   obtain   spend |

1 Before she went to Lancaster University, Susan .................... three 'A' levels.

2 Before she got her degree in biology, she ................... three years in Lancaster.

3 Before she joined Fisons, she ................... on a marketing course.

4 Before she worked at Rootes AgriTec, she ................... disease-resistant rice plants.

5 Before she became a Product Manager at Boots, she ................... remedies for Alzheimer's disease.

| | |
|---|---|
| **NAME:** | Susan Mary GEORGE |
| **ADDRESS:** | 31 Whitstable Road, Canterbury, Kent. |
| **DATE OF BIRTH:** | 9.7.75 |
| **QUALIFICATIONS:** | **Simon Langton Grammar School 1993**<br>GCE 'A' Levels: Maths (Grade B), Biology (Grade B), Chemistry (Grade C)<br><br>**Lancaster University 1993–1996**<br>BSc 2.1 Biochemistry<br><br>**Keele Management College 1997**<br>Eight-week course in marketing |
| **WORK EXPERIENCE:** | **1997–1999 Fisons Pharmaceutical Products**<br>Research assistant responsible for the development of genetically modified disease-resistant rice plants.<br><br>**1999–2000 Rootes AgriTec**<br>Junior executive responsible to Product Manager for commercialising new remedies for Alzheimer's disease.<br><br>**2000– Boots**<br>Product Manager, responsible for over-the-counter medicines. |

**B Regrets**

Susan has been relatively successful but things did not always turn out as she had hoped. Change the verb form in brackets.

1 She wishes she ................... (get) better 'A' level grades.

2 She wishes she ................... (obtain) a distinction at degree level.

3 She wishes she ................... (do) a doctorate.

4 She wishes the marketing course ................... (last) longer than eight weeks.

## Past perfect progressive

**Form**   I / you / we / they had **been working**.   **Had** I / you / we / it **been working**?
He / she / it **had been working**.   **Had** he / she / it **been working**?

I / you / we / they **had** not **been working**.
He / she / it **had** not **been working**.

**Uses**   **1** Talking about events that happened before other events

Like the past perfect simple (see page 18), the past perfect progressive looks back to an event that took place before another past event.

The main difference is that the progressive form emphasises the duration of the first event.

So we normally use the progressive with an expression indicating how long: *for over an hour, for a long time, since 1999*, etc.

**I'd been trying** to get through *for over an hour* before someone answered the phone.
He**'d been thinking** of going abroad *for a long time* and then he got a post in Singapore.
Before they closed down the subsidiary, it **had been losing money** *for years*.

**2** Finished and unfinished activities

Compare:

**a)** When I last saw her she**'d been planning** a new sales strategy.
**b)** When I last saw her she**'d planned** a new sales strategy.

In sentence (a) the planning may or may not have been completed; we don't know whether the new sales strategy was abandoned or not.

In sentence (b) it is clear that the planning had reached an end-point.

Note that we do not use the progressive form with verbs describing permanent states, perception, etc. (For a list see Present simple (1) on page 6.) In such cases we use the past perfect simple.

The man who said there was no future in computers **hadn't understood** their significance.

(NOT *The man who said there was no future in computers hadn't been understanding their significance.)

## Practice

**A Previous and subsequent events**

Complete the following sentences using either the past perfect simple or progressive.

1 My flight from Sydney arrived late because there .................. (be) a bomb alert before the plane took off. When we finally left we .................. (wait) for over five hours.

2 I .................. (work) hard all year so I felt I needed a rest.

3 I .................. (see) the designs before they went on show but they .................. (not impress) me.

4 When I bought my BIP shares, their value .................. (fall) for some time.

5 The merchant bank didn't know that one of their traders .................. (hide) huge losses.

6 The employee was dismissed because he .................. (steal) company property ever since he was taken on.

7 It took me 20 minutes to realise I .................. (look) in the wrong file.

**B Marcel Bich**

Read the extract about Marcel Bich's early career and complete the sentences. If it is not possible to use the past perfect progressive, use the simple form.

Marcel Bich set up in business in 1949 and created France's most successful company and its third best-known brand after Dior and Chanel.

He was educated in Italy as a child, followed by two years at the Lycée Français in Madrid. He completed his secondary education in Bordeaux where he received the nickname 'Baron' – a title that he carried for the rest of his life. At 18, he began selling torches door-to-door and later said that this experience was critical to his entrepreneurial success. At university he studied mathematics and philosophy and after graduation began work as a production manager for an office machine company. He then joined Stephens, a large French pen manufacturer, as a production executive, but the Second World War interrupted his career and when it was over he decided he wanted to set up on his own.

1 Before he died in 1994 he .................. (create) France's most successful company.

2 Before going to Bordeaux he .................. (study) in Italy and Spain.

3 Before he went to university, he .................. (sell) torches door-to-door.

4 Prior to becoming a production manager he .................. (study) maths and philosophy.

5 Before the Second World War broke out he .................. (work) for Stephens as a production executive.

# Combining past and present

## Present perfect simple (1)

**Form**   I / you / we / they **have worked**.
He / she / it **has worked**.

I / you / we / they **have** not **worked**.
He / she / it **has** not **worked**.

**Have** I / you / we / they **worked**?
**Has** he / she / it **worked**?

**Uses**   **1   Talking about present results of past actions**

In this extract, the impact of information technology over the last few years is described in terms of its present significance:

IT **has shaken up** company structures just as much as external markets, says Vanessa Houlder.

To enthusiasts, information technology is forging a productivity revolution. It **has changed** not just the nature of markets and competition. Inside companies, it **has** also **changed** behaviour. It **has broken down** the barriers of geography and time. It **has flattened** organisational structures, eliminating vast numbers of jobs, while making others more demanding and effective.

**2   Announcing news**

The use of the present perfect focuses on current relevance:

Our fax number **has changed**.
We**'ve** just **lowered** our prices.
They **have updated** their website.
The government **has announced** a decrease in corporation tax.
Telecom Italia **has asked** its chief executive to complete negotiations over the company's plans to participate in a new digital pay TV system.

**3   With time adverbs**

We use the present perfect simple to say how long a situation that began in the past has lasted up to the moment of speaking:

He**'s been** vice-president *for* 10 years.
He**'s had** the same job *since* 1996.
She**'s** *always* **been** a creative person.

## Practice

### A Stella McCartney

Choose between the past simple and present perfect. The first one has been done for you.

Stella McCartney, Paul McCartney's daughter, *joined* / ~~has joined~~ the troubled Paris fashion house Chloé barely a year ago. It *took / has taken* [1] her just one year to reverse its fortunes. Previously Chloé *was / has been* [2] virtually invisible as a major force in the world of fashion. But almost single-handedly she *transformed / has transformed* [3] Chloé into the most talked about fashion brand in the world. She *increased / has increased* [4] sales fivefold. Paris *didn't see / hasn't seen* [5] anything like it since the young Yves St Laurent *took / has taken* [6] the city by storm 30 years ago.

When she *was / has been* [7] appointed it *was / has been* [8] clear she *knew / has known* [9] what she *had / has had* [10] to do. 'I want to bridge the gap between the consumer and the press. At the moment fashion is just sort of stuck in the middle.'

So far, Stella *stuck / has stuck* [11] to her philosophy of avoiding outrageous and uncommercial catwalk creations. She *kept / has kept* [12] to the simple philosophy of designing clothes that she or her friends would want to wear. As her best friends are Kate Moss, Naomi Campbell and Yasmin Le Bon, it also brings her big publicity.

### B Market news in brief

Complete these announcements, read out today during a radio programme called *Business in Action*. Complete each one, using these verbs in either the past simple or the present perfect.

> agree   buy   give   issue   slump

In a gigantic deal, BRITISH AMERICAN TOBACCO, the world's second-largest international cigarette maker, ...................[1] to take over ROTHMANS (the fourth-largest) for $8.7 billion.

Shares in MARKS AND SPENCER, Britain's biggest retailer, ...................[2] by more than 10% in the last 24 hours after the firm ...................[3] a profits warning.

Europe's postal market is becoming increasingly competitive. Only weeks after the British government ...................[4] the state-controlled POST OFFICE greater commercial freedom, it ...................[5] Germany's third-largest private carrier. GERMAN PARCEL has a big distribution network and a large stake in GENERAL PARCEL, which operates Europe-wide.

## Present perfect simple (2)

**4 Talking about life experiences**

He**'s done** many jobs in his time. He**'s sold** encyclopaedias, he**'s been** a journalist, he**'s worked** in a shoe factory and now he's a trade unionist.

There is no focus here on *when* he did these things in the past. Only the experiences are important.

**5 With expressions referring to 'time up to now'**

| | |
|---|---|
| **Have** you *ever* **visited** Beijing? | (*ever* = at any previous time up to now) |
| I**'ve** *never* **seen** the Niagara Falls. | (*never* = at no previous time up to now) |
| I**'ve** *already* **had** a word with Bruce. | (*already* = before now) |
| **Hasn't** she **decided** what to do *yet*? | (*yet* = until the present time) |
| We**'ve had** a good year *so far*. | (*so far* = up until now) |
| We**'ve grown** rapidly *over the last few years*. | (= recent years up until now) |

See page 14 for the time expressions which are used with the past simple and not the present perfect.

**6 After** *this is the first / second time*

This is the first time we **have (ever) received** a complaint.
It's only the second time **we've met**.

**7 Referring to a completed event in the future after** *when, as soon as,* **etc.**

I can't make a decision *if* I **haven't received** all the data.
I'll phone you *when* I**'ve received** confirmation. (OR when I **receive**)
I won't make a decision *until* I **have spoken** to the CEO. (OR until I **speak**)
I'll leave *as soon as* I**'ve finished**. (OR as soon as I **finish**)

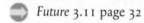 *Future* 3.11 page 32

*I've been on more headed notepaper than you've had business lunches.*

## Practice

**A** Previous experience

Look at Christopher Harvey's CV and ask and answer questions using the present perfect or past simple when appropriate.

| | |
|---|---|
| **EDUCATION** | |
| **1997–1999** | Master's degree in Financial Administration |
| | Project: setting up an import company in Spain |
| **1993–1996** | Business Studies, Henley Management School |
| | Project: market survey of perfume sales in France, Spain and Italy |
| **EMPLOYMENT** | |
| **1996–1998** | Steelcase Strafor (Spain) |
| | Marketing assistant reporting to the marketing director. I was in charge of a dealer development programme involving five other members of staff, responsible for the creation of a mail order catalogue sent to 5,000 customers, creating a database on competing products and planning roadshows for the launch of new products. |
| **1994–1995** | American Cyanamid (Spain) |
| | Export assistant in charge of order processing, customs clearance, dealing with delivery delays. |
| **LANGUAGES** | Spanish: fluent    English: fluent |
| **COMPUTER LITERACY** | Windows, Microsoft Office, QuarkXpress, Photoshop |

Examples:

live abroad?

*Has he ever lived abroad?    Yes, he has. He lived in Spain for a number of years.*

study economics?

*Has he ever studied economics?    No, he hasn't, but he has studied finance.*

| | | | |
|---|---|---|---|
| **1** | be in charge of a team? | **4** | use Excel? |
| **2** | set up a business? | **5** | organise exhibitions? |
| **3** | have direct sales experience? | **6** | deal with export procedures? |

**B** Time words

Sort these words into two categories: *Used with the present perfect* and *Used with the past simple*.

> ago   yet   so far   lately   since   last year   over the last two years
> for the past three weeks   yesterday   at 3 o'clock   during the 1990s

Choose the correct adverb.

**1** I've *yet /already /so far* spoken to Peter about it.

**2** We've made a lot of progress *over the past three years /since three years /during three years*.

**3** We set up *two years ago /during the 1970s /over the last two years*.

## Present perfect progressive

**Form**    I / you / we / they **have been working**.          **Have** I / you / we / they **been working**?
He / she / it **has been working**.                    **Has** he / she / it **been working**?

I / you / we / they **have** not **been working**.
He / she / it **has** not **been working**.

**Uses**    **1**    Talking about continuous activities

We use the present perfect progressive when the focus is on an extended period of time. The situation or activity started in the past and has been in progress for a period until now.

Exports **have been growing** steadily over the past six months.
Foreign earnings **have been moving** ahead to record levels.

The above situations are incomplete; the present perfect simple, on the other hand, tells us that the action has finished.

Compare:

**I've been reading** your proposals.
She**'s been checking** the calculations.          (the focus is on the activities)

**I've read** your proposal.
She**'s checked** the calculations.          (the focus is on their completion)

**2**    Talking about the effect of recent events

'Why are your hands so dirty?' '**I've been trying** to repair my car all afternoon.'
'You look tired!' 'I am. **I've been working** on the report all day.'

What is important is the present result or evidence of this recent activity – in the first example, his hands are dirty; in the second, he looks tired.

**3**    Talking about repeated actions

Compare:

**Have** you **seen** my wife? (I'm looking for her)
**Have** you **been seeing** my wife? (I suspect you're both having an affair)

But we cannot use -ing if we specify the number of occasions or a quantity:

**I've been playing** a lot of golf recently.
**I've played** golf twice this week. (NOT *I've been playing ...)
**I've written** 15 pages today. (NOT *I've been writing ...)

## Practice

**A Recent activities**

Answer these questions with reference to your own situation.

**1** What projects have you been working on recently?

**2** Who have you been working with?

**3** What have you been trying to do, but have not yet succeeded in doing?

**B The effects of recent events**

**1** What explanations could there be for the following?

**a)** Thomas always looks worried and in a hurry. He also finds it difficult to sleep at night.
.............*He's been working too hard.*..........................................

**b)** There are fewer knives and forks in the canteen than a month ago.
...........................................................................

**c)** Top secret company information often gets reported in the press.
...........................................................................

**d)** A lot of dead fish have been found in the river next to the chemicals plant.
...........................................................................

**e)** Pamela was unable to speak any Spanish on her last trip to Madrid but now she can.
...........................................................................

**2** Complete each of these sentences, using the present perfect simple or progressive.

**a)** How long (you / wait)?
...........................................................................

**b)** I (play) tennis four times this week.
...........................................................................

**c)** Look outside. It (rain); the pavement's still wet.
...........................................................................

**d)** 'You look tired.' 'I (drive) all day long.'
...........................................................................

**e)** I (know) John since we were at school together.
...........................................................................

**f)** The government (announce) a drop in unemployment.
...........................................................................

**g)** I (read) a book on negotiating skills but I don't think I'll finish it.
...........................................................................

**h)** He (work) as a consultant for three different firms in the same sector of activity; I think there's a conflict of interest and he should resign.
...........................................................................

**i)** He (work) as a consultant for three different firms in the same sector of activity, but was fired from the first two.
...........................................................................

**Form**   There are a number of ways of making reference to future time. These include:

| | |
|---|---|
| present progressive: | I**'m seeing** Kamil tomorrow. |
| *going to:* | We**'re going to** discuss the new secret deal. |
| present simple: | His plane **gets** to Heathrow at 12.45. |
| *will:* | It **will** probably arrive late owing to air traffic congestion. |
| future perfect simple: | I**'ll have arranged** his hotel accommodation by then. |
| future progressive: | He**'ll be staying** at the Mansion House Hotel. |
| *be* + infinitive: | You **are to tell** nobody of our discussions. |

**Uses**   **1   Talking about plans or arrangements**

We can talk about plans using the present progressive:

I**'m meeting** Mr Wong next week. He**'s arriving** on Tuesday.

**2   Talking about present intentions**

We use *going to* rather than *will* for plans, decisions and firm intentions:

She is **going to** leave in a month's time. (Avoid She ~~will~~ leave ...)
When are you **going to** visit us next? (= When do you intend to ...?)
How much money are you **going to** offer? (= have you decided to offer?)

In general, we prefer a present form when the future event involves some sort of present plan, intention or arrangement. We prefer *will* when we are not focusing on a present idea. Compare:

He**'s going to take** early retirement. (present intention / arrangement)
He**'s taking** early retirement. He'll have a lot more free time. (future situation)

**3   Making predictions**

To make a prediction we can use either *will* or *going to*:

I'm sure you **will** / **are going to** enjoy your visit to our Head Office.

We use *going to* when there is present external evidence for a future event and *will* when we state our own intuitions:

Look at those clouds – it's **going to** rain.
I expect he**'ll** want to stay in the best hotel. (I know what kind of person he is)

**Practice**

**A Ambitions**

Each of the children has an ambition. What do they intend to be when they grow up?

Example:     *Susan is going to be a pilot.*

**1** Susan   **2** Linda   **3** Elizabeth   **4** Michael   **5** Kevin   **6** Sean

**B Predictions**

These forecasts were made by the *Financial Times* at the beginning of 1999. Match the questions to the answers. Did the predictions come true?

**1** Which science will make the news?

**2** Will PCs start talking?

**3** Will international telephone calls cost less?

**4** Will recession hit the UK?

**a)** Yes. The Treasury's forecast of 1–1.5% growth in 1999 will turn out to have been too optimistic and economic activity will slow abruptly in the early part of 1999 as companies shed excess stocks of unsold goods.

**b)** Yes. As the world's telecommunications markets open up, newcomers are using price to take market share from the domestic operator.

**c)** The past year has been dominated by biomedical stories: genes, clones and embryo research. No doubt they will hit the headlines again but there is a good chance that physics, space and astronomy will get more media attention.

**d)** More potent microprocessors and further improvements in the various voice and other technologies underlying computer 'speech' will gradually enable PCs to handle more complex tasks including speech. It probably will not be long before computers speak rather than display messages.

## Future (2)

**4 Making promises or offers**

*Will* is used to make a commitment for the future:

'Could you lend me $50? I**'ll** pay you back tomorrow.'
I don't know if I can finish the job by Friday but I**'ll** do my best.

We use *will* (usually contracted to *'ll*) when an offer is made at the moment of speaking:

'Are you going? I**'ll** give you a lift to the station if you like.'
'I haven't got any means of transport.' 'Don't worry, I**'ll** lend you my car.'

**5 Official calendars and schedules**

For a future event based on an official calendar or schedule we use the present simple. The event is unlikely to change between now and then.

The train **leaves** from Waterloo at 17.59.
Our next planning meeting **is** on Wednesday.

**6 Events completed before a future time**

For events that will be finished before a time in the future we use the future perfect simple:

By the time they arrive we **will have gone home**.
At the end of the year we **will have recovered** our initial investment.

**7 Events happening as a matter of course**

We use the future progressive to describe situations which will arise in the future if things go on as predicted and follow their expected pattern:

No doubt the unions **will be asking** for more money.
She**'ll be retiring** at the end of the year.
Over the next few years average temperatures **will be rising**.

**Practice**

**A Making offers**

How could you offer to help in these situations?

1 'It's really hot and stuffy in here.'

2 'I don't understand this English and it needs translating.'

3 'This desk is too heavy. I can't move it.'

4 'Damn! I've missed the last bus.'

5 'I don't know how I'm going to find time to prepare any slides.'

**B Schedules**

Look at the timetable and ask the questions which elicit the following answers.

| London Heathrow → Birmingham | | | London Heathrow → Manchester | | |
|---|---|---|---|---|---|
| Depart | Arrive | Flight No. | Depart | Arrive | Flight No. |
| 10.40 | 11.25 | BA 3277 | 10.55 | 11.55 | BA 3266 |
| 11.40 | 12.25 | BA 3287 | 11.55 | 12.55 | BA 3276 |

1 ...................................................................................

'At 12.25.'

2 ...................................................................................

'An hour.'

**C Future perfect or future progressive?**

You may not agree with these predictions but you can choose the right verb form anyway!

1 By 2020 the first men ...................................... (land) on the planet Mars.

2 In the next 100 years, the Netherlands ...................................... (disappear) under water.

3 In the second decade of the 21st century people ...................................... (eat) more genetically modified food.

4 By 2030 Chinese ...................................... (become) the language of international scientific communication.

5 Many people ...................................... (live) to over 100 as medical science advances.

## Future (3)

**8 Future events still in progress**

If an event is still in progress at a future time we use the progressive form:

This time next year I**'ll be lying** on a beach in the Bahamas.
During the seminar you**'ll be learning** about negotiation strategies.

The future progressive is also used to talk about arrangements:

During your visit you**'ll be staying** at the Plaza hotel and **meeting** the commercial attaché. You**'ll** also **be visiting** some of the most important potential clients.

**9 Making polite enquiries**

The future progressive can be used to ask a question without giving the impression that we want to influence or direct people's actions. Compare:

**Will** you **be staying** for dinner? (an enquiry about plans)
**Will** you **stay** for dinner? (a request)

**10 Using the present simple after *if, when, until, as soon as***

In time clauses we use the present simple to refer to the future. It is incorrect to use *will* in a time clause:

*If* you **give** us a discount we'll place a bulk order.
Switch off the lights *when* you **leave**.
We won't begin *until* everyone **arrives**.
I'll give you a ring *as soon as* I **get** there.

**11 Stating conditions**

If a condition has to be met before something else can happen, we use the present perfect to refer to the future event in the time clause beginning with *if, when, until, as soon as*:

I can't go *if* I **haven't obtained** a visa.
I'll send you a fax *when* I**'ve made** all the arrangements.
We won't make a decision *until* we **have consulted** everyone.
I'll get back to you *as soon as* I**'ve spoken** to my boss.

**12 Announcing official plans and arrangements**

The infinitive is used to make official announcements:

Lear Corporation is **to axe** 2,800 jobs.
The President is **to visit** Iran next month.

The verb *to be* is often omitted in newspaper headlines:

## Bonn to speed cut in corporate taxes

## CENTRAL AMERICA TO GET $6bn AID

**Practice**

**A** Travel arrangements

A group of travel agents has been invited by a tour operator on a familiarisation trip so that they can find out more about the holidays they sell. Look at the itinerary and complete the tour description using the future progressive.

> ## North India Tour
> DAY 1    BA flight London Gatwick → New Delhi;
> check-in at Whispering Palms Hotel
> DAY 2    Exploration of ancient walled city of Old Delhi; visit to
> Jama Masjid, the largest mosque in India
> DAY 3    Travel by coach to the deserted red sandstone city of Fatehpur Sikri
> DAY 4    Shopping in Agra; Taj Mahal visit at sunset
> DAY 5    Return journey to New Delhi and return flight via Goa

On the first day you'll be flying British Airways to New Delhi. On arrival there'll be a short tour of the city with its wide boulevards and impressive government buildings. We ...................[1] (stay) at the Whispering Palms, which is a pleasant four-star hotel. The next day we ...................[2] (explore) the city of Old Delhi and ...................[3] (visit) Jama Masjid, the biggest mosque in India. Then on the third day we ...................[4] (take) a coach to Fatehpur Sikri, built by the Emperor Akbar as his capital. We check into a hotel and the next day, after some shopping in the bazaar, we ...................[5] (visit) the Taj Mahal at sunset, the best time to see it in its full splendour. On the Friday we ...................[6] (return) to Delhi for a flight to Goa Airport and ...................[7] (transfer) to another hotel for a rest before flying back to London.

**B** *if, when, until, as soon as*

Complete these sentences using appropriate verb forms. (There may be more than one possible answer.)

1 I ................... (get) in touch when I ................... (return) from the Middle East.

2 If they ................... (shut down) the plant, a lot of people ................... (lose) their jobs.

3 We ................... (start) until everyone ................... (be) here.

4 He can't make a decision until he ................... (see) the president.

5 A project to create a bacterial cell from inanimate chemicals ................... (go ahead) as soon as it ................... (receive) approval from an ethics committee.

**C** Announcements

Write suitable headlines for the first lines of these articles.

1 Bill Gates, chief executive of Microsoft, the world's largest software company, has announced initiatives to improve the group's MSN website.

2 BMW has announced that it will now go ahead with a $2.7 billion project to replace Rover's 200 and 400 models.

# Conditionals

## Conditionals (1)

*If* introduces a *condition* – something may or may not happen depending on the circumstances. Conditional sentences have a number of uses.

### 1 Stating a general rule

*If* can be used to say what generally happens when something else happens. Both verbs in this type of sentence are in the present simple tense:

**If** you **order** in bulk you usually **get** a discount.
**If** the paperwork **is** incomplete the goods **are** often held up.

### 2 Speculating about the future

*If* can also be used to speculate about the future consequences of a specific event. In this case, the verb in the second part of the sentence is preceded by *will*.

**If** I **do** an MBA I**'ll improve** my job prospects.
**If** we **break into** the Indian market, our turnover **will increase** substantially.
**If** our main competitor **goes** bankrupt, we**'ll increase** our market share.

The use of the present tense in the first part of the sentence indicates that the situation is *possible*; doing an MBA is feasible, breaking into the Indian market is seen as quite likely, the competitor may well go bankrupt.

Note that it is incorrect to use *will* with the first verb:

NOT *If I will do an MBA ...

### 3 *if* and *unless*

*Unless* often replaces *if* ... + negative expression:

**If** you don't wear a suit and tie you won't be allowed into the club.
You won't be allowed into the club **unless** you wear a suit and tie.

We'll stop the meeting now **if** there is nothing else to discuss.
We'll stop the meeting now **unless** there is something else to discuss.

### 4 Promising and threatening

Conditional statements can function as either promises, warnings or threats. (But note that *unless* cannot be used to make a promise.)

**If** you order now you**'ll** get a free gift. (promise)
We **won't** be able to do business with you **unless** you comply with our ethical policy. (warning)
**Unless** we receive payment by the end of the week we **will** be forced to consider legal action. (threat)

**Practice**

**A It's generally the case**

Match the sentence halves.

1 If the government lowers interest rates,
2 If you want to play golf well,
3 If inflation is high,
4 If the national currency is strong,
5 If you have an offshore bank account,
6 If you pay people peanuts,
7 If a firm doesn't advertise,

**a)** it loses market share.
**b)** people tend not to save.
**c)** it is more difficult to export.
**d)** you get monkeys.
**e)** you have to practise regularly.
**f)** it makes borrowing easier.
**g)** you don't pay income tax.

**B Future consequences**

Write what you will or may do in the following situations.

1 if your car is stolen
2 if a close colleague gets married
3 if you are offered a better-paid job abroad
4 if your firm is taken over by a competitor
5 if you have to give a presentation in English
6 if your computer is infected with a virus

**C *if / unless***

Complete each sentence with either *if* or *unless*.

1 ................... you don't have persistence, you can't be a good salesman.
2 We don't employ people ................... they're flexible and keen to work hard.
3 ................... you do business abroad, it's a good idea to learn about the local culture.
4 ................... you encounter any problems with your mobile phone, we will provide a complete repair service.
5 ................... you call to tell me you're not coming, I'll see you tomorrow afternoon.
6 Don't promise anything ................... you're completely sure.
7 Your presentation will be better ................... you make good eye contact with the audience.
8 ................... you increase sales by over 20%, the company will pay you a performance bonus.

## Conditionals (2)

### 5 Imagining

*If* + past simple is used to refer to less probable situations. *Would / should / could / might* precede the verb in the subordinate clause:

**If** every piece of mail **was** personalised with your company logo or message, your customers **might** be very impressed.
Imagine what **would** happen **if** all the world's stock exchanges **crashed**.
**If** we **hired** a factoring agency we **could** recover our debts more easily.

It is possible to use *if I were* or *if I was* in both formal and informal styles:

If I **was** rich I **would buy** a Ferrari.

### 6 Bargaining

It is common to make hypothetical statements in negotiations. Compare:

**a)** If you **give** us a 5% discount we**'ll** make a firm order of 5,000 units. (this is almost a promise)

**b)** If you **gave** us a 5% discount we**'d** make a firm order of 5,000 units. (this is a more tentative offer)

You may therefore want to use *if* + past verb + *would* as an opening move in a negotiation, in order to test the ground.

### 7 *Provided (that) / so long as / on condition (that)*

When stating a condition it is also possible to use *provided (that), so long as* or *on condition (that)*. It is not necessary to say or write *that*:

**Provided** (**that**) they **don't go** back on their offer, we'll sign the agreement next week.
We'll be happy to work with you **so long as** you pay half of the advertising costs.
We might be able to reduce the number of hours worked **on condition** (**that**) there is an increase in productivity.

## Practice

**A Imagining**

Imagine what would happen in the following (unlikely) situations.

1 If the world was governed by a Communist superpower ...

2 If your husband or wife was offered a good position in Iceland ...

3 If you stood for the presidential elections ...

4 If the sale of alcohol was banned in Europe ...

5 If you were accused of selling your country's military secrets ...

**B Bargaining**

Change the verbs in the brackets as in the example.

1 If you (give) me 90 days to pay I (buy) right now.

   *If you give me 90 days to pay, I'll buy right now.*

2 If you (give) me a special price I (put in) a bigger order.

3 I (take) last year's stock if you (take off) 15%.

4 I (purchase) the equipment if you (throw in) the accessories.

5 How long (you hold) your prices if we (order) today?

6 If I (pay) cash how much discount (you allow)?

**C Negotiating positions**

Expand the prompts to make conditional sentences as in the example.

1 firm orders in advance for one year     reduce the price by 10%?

   *If I gave you firm orders in advance for one year would you reduce the price by 10%?*

2 make a firm order                        agree to split the transport costs 50–50?

3 ensure free maintenance                  buy a new photocopier from us?

4 buy the turbo-diesel model               install air conditioning and a CD-player free of charge?

**D *provided (that), so long as, on condition (that)***

Complete the following sentences, using *provided (that)*, *so long as* or *on condition (that)*.

1 I agree to work seven days a week ...

2 I agree to take a cut in salary ...

3 We agree to make a special delivery ...

## Conditionals (3)

**8** Speculating about the past

When talking about things which did not happen in the past (and the consequences if they had happened) we use *if* + past perfect together with *would / could / might + have* + past participle:

If the price / earnings ratio **had been** higher, I **would have bought** some shares.
If we **had anticipated** the crash, we **wouldn't have lost** so much money.
The merger **could have succeeded if** the management styles **hadn't been** so different.
The presentation **might have been** better **if** she **had felt** more confident.

Note that in American English *would have* is possible in both clauses:

I **would have told** you **if** I **would have known** earlier.

**9** Mixed conditionals

Not all sentences containing *if* follow the same patterns as those presented on this page and on pages 34 and 36. The sequence of tenses depends on the meaning that has to be conveyed.

**If** Robert **wasn't** so lazy he **could have been** promoted. (he is permanently lazy which explains why he failed to get promotion)

**If** you **had set** off earlier you **would be** there by now. (this is true at the moment of speaking; the second part of the sentence does not refer to the past so *would have been* is incorrect)

**If** you **will come** this way I**'ll show** you to Mrs Harvey's office. (*will* can be used after *if* in polite requests)

I**'ll lend** you 1,000 euros **if** it**'ll help** you set up your business. (there is nothing conditional about this sentence; the advantage is the result of the gift of money. Here *if* means *if it is true that*)

We **would** be grateful **if** you **would** send us your payment made out to the order of 'InfoMart'. (a polite request)

**If** the red light **comes on** then **turn off** the machine immediately.

**If** Mrs Olsen **calls, tell** her I'm in a meeting.

**If** you **need** it, **ask** for help. (the verbs in both parts of the sentence are in the present simple tense when giving a warning or instruction or when making an invitation)

**Practice**

**A A negotiation breakdown**

Read the following story and indicate how you would have reacted if you had been in John Dee's or Mrs Han's position.

> John Dee imports microwave ovens from Korea and has been working satisfactorily with the same supplier for five years. Recently he travelled to Korea to meet the supplier and negotiate a reimbursement for a shipment of appliances that John's customers had sent back because of a serious manufacturing defect.
>
> He met the Korean company's representative Mrs Han who insisted she could not compensate John financially but would replace the defective appliances. John refused this offer, saying that this gesture would not in itself be sufficient to restore his reputation with his customers.
>
> John was booked on a plane leaving that afternoon and could see little point in continuing the discussion. He was getting more impatient with the apparent lack of progress and stood up angrily and walked out of the discussion. Mrs Han was embarrassed and did not wish to lose face by asking him to return to the room.
>
> John Dee now buys his microwaves from Taiwan at a higher unit price.

**B Sola-Soda**

Read the text and say if you had been director-general of Sola-Soda Enterprises what would you have done to restore consumer confidence.

> In June 1999 more than 100 people in Spain and two in Italy complained of headaches, dizziness and stomach upsets after drinking canned soft drinks manufactured by Sola–Soda. Subsequently, the authorities in Spain and Italy ordered Sola–Soda products to be withdrawn as a precaution.

**C Mixed conditionals**

Look at the following pairs of sentences and answer the questions about each one.

1 If he hadn't bought a second home in the country he wouldn't be so short of money now.

2 If he had bought a second home in the country he would be short of money now.

  **a)** Did he buy a second home?

  **b)** Is he short of money?

3 If she weren't so busy she would have given you a hand.

4 If she had been busy she wouldn't have given you a hand.

  **c)** Is she busy?

  **d)** Did she help?

# Verb combinations

Verbs are often followed by another verb.

I **enjoy reading**.

I **didn't choose to do** this job.

I **don't want to go**.

You **deserve to get** promotion.

She **denies selling** secrets.

He **doesn't recall meeting** him.

It can be difficult to know whether the second verb is a *to*-infinitive or ends with *-ing*.

## Verb + verb + *-ing*

The *-ing* form focuses on:

a) an action or state before the action of the first verb:

She **admitted taking** a bribe.

He **misses seeing** his wife and children.

She **finished doing** her accounts yesterday.

b) the activity itself. The second verb functions like a noun:

I **dislike travelling**.

She **recommends selling** the shares now.

They **have postponed launching** the new model.

Some common verbs that are followed by *-ing* forms:

| | | | | |
|---|---|---|---|---|
| admit | appreciate | contemplate | give up | involve |
| deny | enjoy | consider | carry on | mean |
| look forward to | mind | justify | can't stand | remember |
| anticipate | resent | warrant | detest | recollect |
| risk | recommend | delay | miss | |
| jeopardise | suggest | put off | avoid | |

## Practice

Verb + verb + *-ing*

1 Match the sentence halves.

1 I'm looking forward to      a) signing anything like that.

2 I don't remember      b) talking for half an hour.

3 He's decided to give up      c) increasing our debt–equity ratio.

4 Borrowing any more money would involve      d) smoking cigars for health reasons.

5 She loves the sound of her voice and carried on      e) seeing you in Milan soon.

2 Using the word in brackets, complete the second sentence so that it has a similar meaning to the first.

a) Travelling doesn't bother me as long as there are no delays. (mind)

I don't ....................................................................................

b) In my job I have to meet many people. (involve)

My job ....................................................................................

c) I certainly did not pass on any trade secrets. (deny)

I firmly ....................................................................................

d) There's a danger we will lose business to our competitors. (risk)

We ....................................................................................

e) I think it would be a good idea to get in touch with the commercial attaché. (suggest)

She ....................................................................................

f) We fully expect to double our turnover in the next two years. (anticipate)

We ....................................................................................

g) He was late so I didn't see him. (miss)

He was late so ....................................................................................

h) Why on earth did you spend so much on entertainment? (justify)

How can you ....................................................................................?

## Verb + *to*-infinitive

The *to*-infinitive form focuses on

a) a purpose:

> She **wishes to ask** you a favour.
> She **intends to complain**.
> They've **decided to go ahead** with the idea.

b) a future situation:

> They are **planning to launch** a takeover bid.
> I've **arranged to see** the financial people tomorrow.
> I **expect to see** them in Taiwan shortly.

Some common verbs that are followed by *to*-infinitive forms:

| | | | | | |
|---|---|---|---|---|---|
| intend | attempt | promise | plan | guarantee | claim |
| mean | try | undertake | arrange | offer | pretend |
| want | hope | forget | seem | fail | |
| wish | expect | remember | appear | neglect | |

## Verb + object + *to*-infinitive

When we want to talk about two actions performed by different people, the verbs are separated by an object:

> He **didn't want** me to attend the meeting. (NOT *He didn't want that I attend ...)
> They **don't allow** you to smoke at work. (NOT *They don't allow that ...)
> A laptop **enables** people **to work** on a plane. (NOT *A laptop enables to work ...)

Some common verbs used with an object and a *to*-infinitive clause:

advise   allow   ask   cause   challenge   choose   defy   enable   encourage
expect   forbid   force   help   inspire   instruct   intend   invite   lead   leave
mean   oblige   order   pay   permit   persuade   prefer   programme   recruit
remind   teach   tell   train   trust   urge   use   warn

## Practice

**A** Verb + *to*-infinitive

Using the word in brackets, complete the second sentence so that it has a similar meaning to the first.

**1** I have every intention of complaining. (intend)

I fully ........................................................................................................

**2** Send them the samples they requested – don't forget, will you? (remember)

Please ........................................................................................................

**3** We will provide a 24 hour-a-day-hot line. (undertake)

We

........................................................................................................

**4** I anticipate receiving an answer soon. (expect)

I ........................................................................................................

**5** If you like we can send a replacement. (offered)

They have ........................................................................................................

**6** She should have told them of the potential problem. (neglected)

She ........................................................................................................

**7** I'm not sure, but I think there is a bug in the program. (appears)

There ........................................................................................................

**8** She says she has the necessary authority. (claims)

She ........................................................................................................

**B** Verb + object + *to*-infinitive

The words in the following sentences are in the wrong order. Rewrite them in the correct order.

**1** me she to in myself taught believe

**2** dirty they me to their do work paid

**3** he perform a certain programmed robot to number tasks the of

**4** federation the the rates cut Minister to interest urged employers'

**5** the from expertise to enabled joint benefit our us partner's venture

## Verb + object + verb + *-ing*

**1 Some verbs are used with an object and a second verb ending in *-ing***

Verbs used in this way include:

catch  describe  discover  feel  find  hear  imagine
keep  leave  like  listen to  notice  observe  prevent (from)
save  see  send  set  show  watch

Her comment **set** me **thinking**.
Outsourcing would **save** you **spending** money on permanent staff.
The white knight **prevented** the company from **being** taken over.

**2 Verbs of perception**

| *Not all of the action is seen or heard* | *All of the action is seen or heard* |
| --- | --- |
| I **saw** a man **stealing** some clothes from a store. | I **saw** a man **steal** some clothes from a store. |
| He **watched** the crowd **leaving** the stadium. | He **watched** the crowd **leave** the stadium. |
| I **heard** a door **banging** repeatedly. | I **heard** a door **bang** once and then nothing. |

## Verb + infinitive without *to*

A few verbs used in second position do not take *to*. These are *let, make* and *have* (in the sense 'cause to happen'):

We **let** them have a 10% discount. (NOT *let them to have)
Don't **make** me laugh. (NOT *make me to laugh)
Could you **have** Mrs Smith bring in the coffee now? (NOT *have Mrs Smith to bring)

## Verb + *it* + object clause

When the object of a verb is a clause, *to*-infinitive or *-ing* structure, we use *it* after the verb to introduce the clause:

I find **it** impossible to understand their culture.
The government regard **it** as unnecessary to harmonise taxation.
She feels **it** is necessary to send a copy to absolutely everyone.
He found **it** worthwhile visiting the overseas subsidiaries.

## Practice

**A  Verbs of perception**

There was a break-in at the headquarters of a company and the nightwatchman has made a statement to the police saying what he saw and heard.

Complete the statement using these verbs.

> have   go through   feel   beat   move   whisper   come   lie   shout

I have worked as a nightwatchman here for six years and there has never been any trouble. But on the night in question at about 3am I was looking at the closed circuit TV screens in my room and saw someone .................[1] about in one of the offices. So I took my torch and went to investigate. I decided not to take the lift because an intruder would hear it .................[2] so I walked upstairs as quietly as I could. I stopped on the second floor and listened to my heart .................[3]. I took out my revolver and took off the safety catch. At that moment I imagined myself .................[4] a gun battle and I couldn't prevent myself from .................[5] afraid. I imagined myself .................[6] in a pool of blood in the deserted building. Then I continued up to the third floor and walked down the corridor. I could hear two people .................[7] to each other. I walked on, and through an open door I observed two masked men .................[8] the contents of the CEO's desk. Then after about 30 seconds – but it seemed like an eternity – I heard someone .................[9] something for a split second, then everything went blank.

**B  Verb patterns**

Correct the errors in these sentences.

1  I find impossible to work with him.
2  They made us to work extremely hard in my previous job.
3  She never let me to take any decisions.
4  Could you have Mr Clarke to prepare some statistics?
5  She's finding difficult to get used to the climate.
6  I feel is necessary to delegate more of the work.

## Verb + *for* + *to*-infinitive

Some verbs are followed by the preposition *for* and its object, then an infinitive:

He **arranged for** his secretary *to drive* him to the airport.
I **waited for** him *to get back* in touch.
They **called for** the Union *to reconsider* its strike action.

These verbs can be used in this way:

appeal  apply  arrange  ask  call  opt
pay  plead  vote  wait  wish  yearn

## Verb + possessive + verb + *-ing*

It is possible to introduce a possessive pronoun or a genitive between the first and second verb. Thus *Please forgive me for asking* can be reformulated more formally as *Please forgive **my** asking*. Other verbs that follow this pattern are:

That would **entail** our making a concession.
This will **save** our wasting time.
They have **suggested** his going to the symposium.
He's **looking forward to** our coming.
'I don't **mind** your being killed, but I **object to** your being taken prisoner.' (Lord Kitchener to the Prince of Wales, on his asking to fight during the 1914–18 war)

## Special cases

Certain verbs are followed by either an infinitive or another verb + *-ing,* but the choice leads to a change in the meaning:

I will never **forget** meeting Princess Diana. (= I will always remember)
I sometimes **forget** to wear my badge. (= fail to remember)

I **mean** to see her later this week. (= I intend to)
I could get a better job but it would **mean** moving (= involve)

He was an alcoholic but **stopped** drinking. (= ceased)
He **stopped** to have a drink on the way back home. (= in order to)

She **remembered** to turn off her headlights. (= she didn't forget)
She **remembers** turning off her headlights. (= she has a clear memory of this)

Why don't you **try** giving the staff greater autonomy? (= experiment and see what happens)
He **tried** to learn car maintenance but gave up. (= attempted / made the effort)

## Practice

**A** Verb + *for* + *to*-infinitive

Match the sentence halves in order to make logical sentences.

1 The opposition party has called for
2 The conference organiser has arranged for
3 The production manager has been waiting for
4 The shareholders voted for
5 Her father paid for

a) the company to increase its share capital.
b) the spare parts to arrive.
c) the prime minister to resign.
d) her to go to an American university.
e) the delegates to stay in a four-star hotel.

**B** Special cases

Use the correct form of the verb in brackets to complete these extracts.

**1**

The German Chancellor intervened yesterday in a dispute with the energy industry over plans to stop ..................... (use) nuclear power.

**2**

In 1996 five big US networks donated airtime to political candidates for the first time but a survey of registered voters showed that most of them did not remember ................... (see) the broadcasts.

**3**

Apparently, the commissioner meant ............. (inform) the investigators of the secret payments into a special fund but was persuaded not to do so.

**4**

Embarrassment yesterday as the wife of the prime minister attended the presentation of a football trophy. Unfortunately someone forgot ........... (tell) the photographers and the event had to be reprogrammed.

**5**

It could be that there is no crisis of faith in managers. It may simply be that suddenly everyone wants to be a management consultant or, failing that, an investment banker. If all those MBAs really do mean ............. (work) for McKinsey, Boston Consulting Group, Goldman Sachs and all the rest, good luck to them. But if they believe that being a consultant or investment banker will mean ................... (have) a balanced life with plenty of time for family and friends, they may be in for a rude shock.

## Passives (1)

**Form**    We form the passive by using the appropriate tense of *to be* + a past participle:

Uranium **is mined** in Australia.
The company **was set up** in 1997.
A new extension **is being built**.
The company **has been taken** over.

It is also possible to use the passive with a modal verb:

The goods **will** be sent by rail.
The shipment **may** be delayed.
Tenders **should** be submitted in triplicate.
Helmets **must** be worn.

The subject of a passive verb corresponds to the object of an active verb:

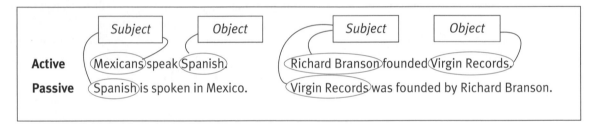

| | Subject | Object | Subject | Object |
|---|---|---|---|---|
| **Active** | Mexicans speak Spanish. | | Richard Branson founded Virgin Records. | |
| **Passive** | Spanish is spoken in Mexico. | | Virgin Records was founded by Richard Branson. | |

**Uses**    **1**   Focusing on the action

We use a passive construction when we are not interested in who performs an action or it is not necessary to know:

The date **was changed**.
The missing file **has been found**.
He **has been promoted** to the post of Sales Director.

If we also want to mention who performs the action we can use a phrase beginning with *by*:

The decision **was taken** *by the committee*.
The missing file **has been found** *by one of the cleaners*.

**2**   Focusing on information

In a passive sentence, the grammatical subject receives the focus:

The visiting delegation **was met** by the president at the airport.

Here the visiting delegation, rather than the president, is the centre of interest.

## Practice

**A** Passive verb forms

Match the sentence halves appropriately.

1 Your enquiry            **a)** has been confirmed.

2 Make sure that your mobile phone        **b)** has been credited to your account.

3 All tenders and supporting documents      **c)** has not yet been printed.

4 Your hotel booking            **d)** is switched off during important meetings.

5 As requested, the sum of $75,000       **e)** must be returned by 31 March.

6 The full conference programme        **f)** is being dealt with.

**B** Focusing on the action

Make these sentences passive. Only use *by* if it is necessary to say who did the action.

1 Karl Marx wrote *Das Kapital*.

2 They are repairing your car now.

3 Steve Jobs founded Apple Computers.

4 The board will discuss the proposal.

5 Did anyone inform Mrs Wilson?

6 They make Renault cars in Slovenia.

7 They have transferred him to the New York office.

8 The princess opened the new conference centre.

9 They had made a full investigation.

10 I didn't realise someone was listening to my telephone conversations.

**C** Focusing on information

Read the following and rewrite the information, changing the focus as in the example.

### Dealing with messages

Written documents and messages land on your desk all the time
and you need to process them efficiently. Here are a few tips.

- You should read through documents quickly and absorb their main information content.
- If you need to file a written document you can write the file name on the document
- If a written message requires action, you should make a note, for example on a Post-It®.
- You should dispose of all messages once you have dealt with them.

**Dealing with messages**

Written documents and messages land on your desk all the time and ...*need to be processed*........
efficiently. Here are a few tips.

- Documents ......................[1] quickly and their main information content ..........................[2].
- If ............................................[3] the file name ....................................................[4].
- If a written message requires action, ........................................[5], for example on a Post-It®.
- ...........................................................................................................[6]

**Passives (2)**

### 3 Describing a process or procedure

We use the passive because we are more concerned with the process itself than who carries it out. For example, here is a description of the wine-making process:

Wine **is made** from the fermented juice of grapes. Grapes **are picked** at optimum sugar / acidity levels. After picking, the grapes **are taken** to the winery, **de-stemmed** and **crushed** in a variety of presses. The juice **is** then **clarified** by settling or by centrifuge, yeast and sugar **are added** and the wine **is left** to ferment in tanks. When fermentation **is finished** the wine **is poured** into a clean tank to stabilise. It **can** then **be filtered** and **bottled** and left to mature.

### 4 Writing in a formal style

When writing in a formal style (e.g. reports, minutes of meetings) we often choose an impersonal style by using the passive and beginning sentences with *it*.

**It was agreed** to increase the share capital.
**It was considered** to be an unacceptable alternative.
**It has** now **been decided** to postpone the proposed construction.

Another common way of reporting what is said or thought is to use *it* + passive + *that*-clause

**It was agreed that** the share capital should be increased.
**It was felt that** some economies had to be made.

Other verbs used in this pattern include:

announce    claim    discover    estimate    expect    know
mention    propose    recommend    suggest    think    understand

### 5 Reporting unconfirmed information

When the statement is speculative we use the passive of *say, think, consider, believe* followed by an infinitive. This structure is common in newspaper reporting:

The minister **is said to be** in favour of decreasing corporation tax.
The board **is thought to be** in favour of a merger.
He **is considered to be** the best chairman the company has ever had.
The terrorists **are believed to want** a new ceasefire.

**Practice**

**A** Check your understanding

Are these sentences true or false?

1 Passives are used when we are interested in who has done something rather than what is done.

2 Passives are used when the focus is on what is done rather than the people who perform the action.

3 The object of an active verb corresponds to the subject of a passive verb.

4 Passives are common in an informal style.

5 The passive is often used to describe the stages of a process.

**B** Active or passive?

Complete this advertisement, using either the active or the passive as appropriate.

> **Communicado**'s presentation skills training courses ....................[1] (tailor) to each client's individual needs, so the main focus is on the type of presentations that ....................[2] (give) by the participants in their everyday working lives. Courses ....................[3] (conduct) either on a one-to-one basis or in groups. They are highly participative and ....................[4] (design) to be enjoyable as well as instructive.
>
> **Communicado** ....................[5] (encourage) clients to ....................[6] (build) on their existing social communication skills. Through a number of interesting techniques we ....................[7] (show) clients how time can ....................[8] (save) in preparation, how body language can ....................[9] (use) to maximum effect and how visual aids can ....................[10] (create) for maximum impact.
>
> For more details on how **Communicado** can ....................[11] (help) your company improve its business presentations, call **0800 222 4567** now.

**C** Describing a process

The following passage describes the production of paper. Put the words in brackets into the appropriate form, using the passive when necessary.

> **From trees to pulp**
>
> The trees ....................[1] (transport) to the paper mill by lorry, train or ship. First the bark ....................[2] (remove). This ....................[3] (burn) at a later stage so that energy can ....................[4] (generate) for the paper-making process. Then the logs ....................[5] (cut) into chips and ....................[6] (cook) under high pressure for four hours to make paper pulp. Next the pulp ....................[7] (bleach) to ....................[8] (remove) dirt spots and ....................[9] (improve) its ageing properties.
>
> **From pulp to paper**
>
> The manufacturing process also ....................[10] (require) chemicals to strengthen the paper. The fibres ....................[11] (mix) with additives and ....................[12] (dilute) with water. This mixture ....................[13] (spray) onto the paper machine where it ....................[14] (press), then ....................[15] (dry) and ....................[16] (wind) onto one large reel which ....................[17] (weigh) up to 20 tons. Each part of the process ....................[18] (control) by computers which automatically ....................[19] (correct) any errors.

# Modal verbs (expressing subjective viewpoints)

**Form**  A modal always comes before another verb:

> You **must go**.

A modal is not followed by *to*:

> NOT *You must to go.

The form of a modal never changes; there is no *s* on the third person, no *-ing* form, no past tense:

> NOT *You musts go, *musting, *You musted.

Questions are formed by inverting the modal and the subject:

> **Must you** go?

Modals are not used together:

> NOT *She will must go.

**Uses**  Modal verbs are auxiliary verbs that express the speaker's judgement about the likelihood or desirability of a situation. All modals can be used to talk about probability or possibility; modals can also be used to express interpersonal meanings such as obligation or willingness.

## Ability

**1  Saying that someone knows how to do something**

We use *can* to say that someone is able / not able to do something:

Our new divisional manager **can** speak four languages fluently.
He **can't** drive, he's never learnt how to.

We also use *can* to say that machines are able to perform certain tasks:

The new photocopier **can** print out a whole book in less than five minutes.

**2  Talking of a past ability**

He **could** play the piano when he was five years old.

This sentence refers to an ability that was not limited to just one occasion. If we want to speak of one event we use *managed to* or *was able to*:

After six hours of negotiation, we finally **managed to** make some progress. (NOT *we could)
After six hours of negotiation, we **were** finally **able to** make some progress.

The negative form is, however, possible for just one occasion:

We **couldn't** get tickets for the opera – they were all sold out.

**3  Indicating disapproval when something is or was not done**

She **could** make more of an effort. (= she is able to, but doesn't)
You **could have told** me beforehand – I needed to know. (= you were able to, but didn't)

**Practice**

**A Abilities**

Match the personal qualities with the abilities on the right.

| *If you* | *you can* |
|----------|-----------|
| **1** are computer literate | **a)** work well on your own. |
| **2** are trilingual | **b)** use different types of software. |
| **3** are good at mental arithmetic | **c)** solve problems rationally. |
| **4** are autonomous | **d)** be a good leader. |
| **5** have a creative personality | **e)** calculate quickly in your head. |
| **6** have a logical mind | **f)** speak three languages. |
| **7** are decisive and people accept your authority | **g)** bring new ideas to projects. |

**B Past abilities**

Complete the sentences using either *could* or *managed to.*

**1** After a lot of discussion we ................... strike a deal.

**2** He was a brilliant linguist and ................... speak over a dozen languages fluently.

**3** I thought I was going to miss the plane but I ................... get to the airport on time.

**4** When I was younger I ................... run several kilometres without feeling tired.

**5** She ................... find a good job despite her lack of formal qualifications.

**6** When we lived near the beach we ................... go swimming every day.

**7** She ................... have left me a message – how was I supposed to know?

**C Indicating disapproval**

React to these situations using *could have.*

**1** Why didn't she ring to tell me she would be late?

**2** She had the facts and figures but left me in the dark.

**3** It wasn't worth us taking a taxi, the station was within walking distance.

**4** It took six days for the letter to arrive and we both have e-mail.

## Obligation, prohibition

**1  Saying what is compulsory**

We use *must* or *has / have to* to indicate what is compulsory in the present and future:

'Any change in taxation **must** be fair, fiscally responsible and **must** avoid simply shifting the burden from the rich to the middle class,' the president said.
All travellers to China **have to** be in possession of a visa.

*Must* can also be used in reported speech:

The London Chamber of Commerce and Industry said the government **must** act to tackle the capital's traffic problems.

If something was necessary or obligatory in the past we use *had to* and we use *will have to* for the future:

When we lived in São Paulo we **had to** learn some Portuguese.
We **will have to** evaluate the new procedure regularly.

The absence of future obligation is expressed by *will not / won't have to*:

If you open a bank account in the Bahamas you **won't have to** pay income tax.

**2  Imposing an obligation on ourselves**

We prefer to use *must* when we oblige ourselves to do something. We prefer *have to* when the obligation is imposed by other people or external circumstances:

I **must** remember to get in touch with Mr Gonzales, I keep forgetting.
I **must** buy my wife a present before I go home.
We **have to** wear a uniform at work, it's not our choice.
I enjoy going to conferences unless I **have to** make a presentation.

**3  Freedom to choose**

If you *do not have to* do something, there is no obligation – you are free to act:

I can work from home so I **don't have to** go into the office very often.

**4  Saying that something is prohibited**

We use *must not* (NOT *do not have to) to say that something is forbidden or very unacceptable:

Passengers **must not** smoke during take-off.
You **mustn't** enter a joint venture unless both parties benefit from the deal.

*Cannot* and *may not* are also used if something is forbidden because of a rule or a law:

Retailers **cannot / may not** sell below cost price in some countries.

**Practice**

**A Rules and regulations**

Complete these sentences so that they are true for your country. Use *have to*, *don't have to* and *must not*.

1 You ................... carry a gun.

2 You ................... pay to use buses and trams.

3 You ................... vote if you are over 18.

4 You ................... drink alcohol at work.

5 You ................... pay to drive on a motorway.

6 You ................... declare income earned abroad.

7 You ................... wear a seat belt when driving a car.

**B Rules at work**

Complete these sentences so that they are true for your job situation. Use *have to*, *don't have to* and *must not*.

1 You ................... take home company equipment.

2 You ................... wear a badge.

3 You ................... wear a tie, if you are a man.

4 You ................... wear jeans at work.

5 You ................... clock in when you arrive.

6 You ................... wear a dress or a suit, if you are a woman.

**C Signs and notices**

What can you say about these signs using *have to*, *don't have to*, *must* and *must not*?

1  2  4  7

3 5 6

## Possibility

### 1 Expressing possibility

We use *can* to say that something is possible and *cannot* or *could not* if something is impossible:

Mathematics **can** be really interesting.
In some cases, customs clearance **can** be difficult to obtain.
You **can't** fly to Dover – there isn't an airport.
Protectionism **can't** be the final answer to a country's economic problems.
I **couldn't** tell you exactly what our turnover is but it's over £100 million.

If a situation is possible but it is not certain that it will happen or be possible, we use *could*:

A lot of accidents at work **could** be avoided.
If we outsourced more we **could** save a lot of money.

### 2 Saying something was possible in the past

We use either *could* or *used to be able to*:

Twenty years ago you **could** walk in the fields but they've all been built on now.
You **used to be able to** put coins in telephone boxes but not now.

We use *could not* or *couldn't* if something was impossible:

Twenty years ago you **couldn't** buy a computer as cheaply as you can now.

This could be reformulated as:

Twenty years ago you **didn't use to be able to** buy a computer as cheaply as you can now.

### 3 Talking about past opportunities

A past opportunity which was not fulfilled is expressed using *could have* and a past participle:

She **could have gone** to Harvard but she went to Yale instead.
He **could have been** a Member of Parliament but he preferred to stay out of politics.

*He could have been a member of Parliament but he preferred to stay out of politics.*

## Practice

### A *can*

Make appropriate sentences from this table using *can*.

| | | | |
|---|---|---|---|
| Learning a foreign language<br>Entertaining overseas customers<br>Being in charge of a new project<br>Setting up in business<br>Negotiating a contract | can | occasionally<br>sometimes<br>often | be | hard work<br>good fun<br>challenging<br>a waste of time<br>painful<br>boring |

### B *could / couldn't*

Rewrite these sentences using *could* or *couldn't*.

1 If we diversified we would be able to offer a wider range of products.

2 If I had stayed in the States I would have been able to get a better job.

3 In the 1980s it was possible to make a fortune as a 'golden boy'.

4 She had an opportunity to do an MBA but decided it was too much work.

5 Thirty years ago you used to be able to buy cigarettes in packets of five.

6 Before privatisation it wasn't possible to buy shares in British Telecom.

### C Missed opportunities

Read the following story and list the missed opportunities using *could have*.

As a young man Peter Metro was a gifted musician who once had a record in the top 20. But he decided to abandon music and study ocean engineering at Florida Atlantic University instead. After four years there he graduated and was offered a research post in the faculty. But by that time he had decided he wanted to see the world and spent a year travelling Europe. In Italy he happened to meet the film director Roberto Bellini who offered him a role in his latest film, but he turned it down because he had just accepted a job with a small firm specialising in the construction of racing catamarans. One day the famous skipper Chris Dickson asked him to sail with him during the Admiral's Cup but Peter decided not to because he was too busy.

## Likelihood

A number of modal verbs are used to express degrees of certainty, according to the speaker's perception of the situation.

**1  100% certain**

The 21st century **will** be very different from the preceding 1,000 years. (an obvious prediction)
Economics **will** never be a precise science. (a general truth)

**2  Very certain (based on deduction)**

You **must** be very tired after such a long flight.
That **can't** be Rowena's car – she's driving to London today.

**3  Probably**

You **may well** have a point there.
Interest rates **could well** go up by a whole percentage point.
We **should** arrive before lunch if there's not too much traffic.

**4  Likely (based on speculation)**

The decision this week by the Gulf Co-operation Council to allow national banks to set up branches in each other's countries is a first step towards banking liberalisation. It **could** also help efforts by banks to expand. The move **could** open up the large Saudi and Kuwaiti banking markets to other Gulf banks.

The firm **may** be forced to make a number of employees redundant in the coming months but the situation **may** improve in the longer term.

*Might* suggests less certainty:

The president **might** survive the scandal but his chances look pretty slim.

**5  Highly unlikely / impossible**

You **won't** know Agnes – she's our new marketing person.
We **can't** meet such a short deadline.

**Practice**

**A  Degrees of likelihood**

This text deals with the likelihood of an earthquake in the San Francisco area. Decide where each of the phrases (a–h) fits into the passage.

The next big earthquake in the Bay area may come sooner than you think. There is a 67 percent chance of at least one earthquake of magnitude 7 or larger in the San Francisco Bay area between now and 2020. Such an earthquake ....................[1].

Some scientists believe that the 67 percent probability estimate ....................[2]. They have noted several instances of pairs of earthquakes of magnitude 6.5 or larger in northern California, and they are concerned that the Loma Prieta earthquake ....................[3]. Other fault segments in northern California ....................[4]. Therefore it seems prudent to consider the 67 percent chance of a large earthquake within the next 20 years as a minimum estimate.

Future studies are also likely to produce additional data that ....................[5]. However, the major conclusions are not likely to change. Scientists agree that:

- Earthquakes of magnitude 7 and larger are highly likely within the Bay area during the next few decades.
- Each of these events ....................[6] because each will probably be located closer to densely populated areas.
- Action is needed now to reduce the damage and the number of deaths that ....................[7] even if this ....................[8].

From *United States Geological Survey*

**a)** might also be capable of producing large earthquakes

**b)** may be too low

**c)** could cause more damage than the Loma Prieta quake

**d)** will result in changes in probability estimates

**e)** could strike at any time, including today

**f)** could be the first quake of such a pair

**g)** may involve significant expense

**h)** could result from future major earthquakes

**B  Expressions of likelihood**

What other expressions of likelihood are there in this passage?

## Permission, suggestions, offers

### 1 Asking for and giving permission

*Can* is used to ask for and give permission:

'**Can** I use your mobile phone?' 'Sure, you **can** – go ahead.' / 'No, you **can't**.'

*May* and *could* are also used to ask for permission, but not to refuse permission. They are more formal than *can*:

'**May** I use your password?' 'No, I'm afraid you can't.' (NOT *I'm afraid you may not.)
'**Could** I come back later?' 'No, I don't think that'll be possible.' (NOT *No, you couldn't.)

If we want to talk about permission for a future action we use the verb *allow* or *permit*:

They won't **allow** / **permit** you to travel alone. (NOT *They won't can ...)

### 2 Making suggestions

I think you **should** upgrade your computer.
You **might** want to look at the new Compaq model.
Or you **could** add extra memory to your existing machine.
**Shall** I look at what it would cost?

### 3 Offering

**Can** we give you a lift into town?
**Would** you like me to give you a hand?
**Shall** I give you a hand? (Note that this is an offer in the present, not for the future.)
**I'll** give you a hand if you like. (Note that the offer is made by *'ll* not *will* or *shall*.)
**Let me know** if you need any help.

If you want to make an offer in a persuasive way you can use *must*. (Note that there is no obligation here!)

You **must** come and visit me sometime.

 *Suggesting* page 140

**Practice**

**A** **Permission, suggestions or offers?**

Decide if the following are requests for permission, suggestions or offers.

**1** Shall we go for lunch?

**2** May I sit here?

**3** Shall I give you a lift into town?

**4** Can I borrow the car this weekend?

**5** Could I use your mobile phone?

**6** You might like to check the exchange rate first.

**7** Would you like us to send you a catalogue?

**8** In my opinion you should sell your shares now.

**9** Are you hot? I'll switch on the air conditioning if you like.

**B** **Offers and suggestions**

Complete the dialogue with these expressions.

> Do you need any help     I'll give you     Shall I hold the door open
> Would you like me     We must get together

**A** It's been wonderful seeing you. ..................[1] some time.

**B** Yes, that'd be very nice.

**A** ..................[2] with your baggage?

**B** No, thanks. I can manage.

**A** Are you sure? ..................[3] for you?

**B** Yes, please.

**A** ..................[4] to call a taxi?

**B** No, thanks. I'll walk. It's not far.

**A** No, you can't possibly. Your cases are heavy. ..................[5] a lift. It won't take me two minutes to get the car.

**B** Well, thank you very much. It's really very kind of you.

**A** Not at all. It's my pleasure.

## Willingness, refusal, promises, threats, typical behaviour

### 1 Asking people if they don't mind

We use *will* or *would* to make a polite request or to ask someone if they are willing to assist:

**Will** you come this way?      **Will** you sign here, please?
**Would** you do me a favour?      **Would** you tell him that Mr Harvey phoned?

But a request can also function as a command:

**Will** you be here at 9 o'clock sharp, please?

### 2 Insisting

*Will* can mean 'to insist on doing something' even if it is inadvisable:

If you **will** smoke two packets a day, it's not surprising you've got a persistent cough.

### 3 Refusing

If you want to say that you are unwilling to do something, you can use *will not* or *won't*:

I **will not** tolerate her behaviour any longer.

Other people or things can also show unwillingness:

The car **won't** start.      He **won't** ever do what I tell him to do.

### 4 Promising

If you make a firm commitment to do something in the future you use *will*:

We **will** do everything in our power to satisfy your needs.

However, the promise may have a negative impact and is therefore interpreted as a threat:

Unless you comply we **will** be forced to initiate legal proceedings.

### 5 Routine behaviour or general truths

Most days **I'll** get home at about 7.30pm but quite often later.
Murphy's law states that if something can go wrong it **will** go wrong.

*Would* is used to talk about actions that happened frequently in the past:

Our previous chairman **would** always begin the annual general meeting with a joke.

## Practice

**A** Uses of *will* and *would*

Which of the following uses of *will* indicate willingness (W), refusal (R), a promise (P), a threat (T) or typical behaviour (TB)? Write the appropriate letter in the space provided.

**1** I'll make sure John is informed. ....................

**2** Oil will float on water. ....................

**3** She won't listen, she's so stubborn. ....................

**4** Patrick will keep on asking stupid questions. ....................

**5** I'll take your calls for you while you're out. ....................

**6** Either I get the job or I'll leave the company. ....................

**7** Will you call him back when you've got a moment? ....................

**8** I've changed the battery but my mobile phone still won't work. ....................

**9** She will always be the first person to arrive on a Monday morning. ....................

**10** If you don't sign the new contract we'll have to move you to another post. ....................

**11** Would you put your name and company in the visitors' book, please? ....................

**12** Before the use of computers we would have to record all our data on card index files. ...............

**B** *will, won't* or *would*?

Rewrite the sentences using *will*, *won't* or *would*.

**1** Accidents inevitably happen.

**2** I promise to do my best.

**3** He refuses to accept her authority.

**4** If you don't pay, legal action is certain to be taken.

**5** A fanatic is someone who can't change his mind and refuses to change the subject. (Winston Churchill)

**6** If you insist on being rude how can you expect people to like you?

**7** He used to smoke a large cigar before making an important decision.

**8** The product with the better-known brand name inevitably sells better than the other.

# Multi-word verbs

Multi-word verbs are very frequent in English. There are over 3,000 of them with over 5,000 meanings! They are created when a verb, often a very common one such as *come, get, give, go, make, put, run, take, turn,* combines with 'particles' like *at, away, down, in, off, on, up* and so on.

## Types of multi-word verbs

**1  Without an object**

The truck **broke down** on the freeway.
We've **scaled down** the size of the project.
I'll be **tied up** all day so I can't see her until tomorrow.

**2  With an object – separable**

Adverb particles can go before or after noun objects:

We've **brought forward** the meeting.
We've **brought** the meeting **forward**.
Could you **switch off** the computer?
Could you **switch** the computer **off**?

However, the particle cannot be used before a pronoun:

We've **brought** it **forward**. (NOT *We've brought forward it.)

Note that if the noun phrase is long, it is very unusual to separate the verb and particle. The second sentence below is unacceptable:

We've **narrowed** the number of choices **down** to three.
NOT *We've narrowed the number of choices down that we think are feasible to three.

**3  With an object – inseparable**

Some verbs are followed by a preposition. In this case, the preposition goes before the object:

We'll have to **look into** the matter. (NOT *look the matter into)
I'm **counting on** your support. (NOT *counting your support on)

**4  With an adverb particle and a preposition**

She is trying to **back out of** our agreement.
The austerity measures **came in for** a lot of criticism.
We're not prepared to **put up with** her absenteeism any longer.

## Practice

**A With or without an object?**

Decide which of these sentences doesn't need an object to complete it. If it does, choose an appropriate sentence ending from those on the right.

<table>
<tr><td>1 Neither of the opponents would give in</td><td>a) a lot of abuse.</td></tr>
<tr><td>2 Our policy is never to turn away</td><td>b) a new name for the brand.</td></tr>
<tr><td>3 She's thought up</td><td>c) a customer.</td></tr>
<tr><td>4 A number of reasons can account for</td><td>d) a meeting with the director.</td></tr>
<tr><td>5 She came in for</td><td>e) the change.</td></tr>
<tr><td>6 I was completely taken in</td><td></td></tr>
<tr><td>7 I wonder when it will turn up</td><td></td></tr>
<tr><td>8 I don't understand what you're getting at</td><td></td></tr>
<tr><td>9 Crowds of people were turned away</td><td></td></tr>
<tr><td>10 Try to fix up</td><td></td></tr>
</table>

**B Separable or inseparable?**

Decide which of these sentences are acceptable (A) and which are unacceptable (U).

Example:

We brought the meeting forward.   .A..

We brought forward the meeting.   .A..

We brought forward it.   .U.

1 We've sent off the catalogue to the printer's.   .....

2 We've sent it off to the printer's.   .....

3 We've sent off it to the printer's.   .....

4 She wants to put off the meeting until next week.   .....

5 She wants to put it off until next week.   .....

6 She wants to put the meeting off until next week.   .....

7 Could you go over the report again for me?   .....

8 Could you go the report over for me?   .....

9 Could you go it over for me?   .....

10 We're trying to break into a new market.   .....

11 We're trying to break a new market into.   .....

12 We're trying to break it into.   .....

13 We're going to phase out the old model.   .....

14 We're going to phase the old model out.   .....

15 We're going to phase it out.   .....

## Understanding multi-word verbs (1)

Many multi-word verbs are easy to understand:

What time do you **get up**?          Could you **turn down** the volume?

In these examples the particle has an easily interpreted meaning. Others are not so easy:

They **got up** a petition to protest against the job cuts. (= organised)
She applied for the post but was **turned down**. (= refused)

It can help if you understand the meaning of the particle which combines with a verb.

**1** *up*

**a)** increasing

We need to **build up** stocks in case there's a strike.
The economy is beginning to **pick up** again.
She's opened a new bank account and wants to **save up** for a new car.

**b)** advancing / coming closer

I'm trying to **make up** the time I lost when I was sick.
It's difficult to **keep up** with all the latest developments.
The car **drew up** beside us and the driver asked for directions.

**c)** inventing

The advertising agency is trying to **think up** a brilliant new slogan.
Where did you **dream up** that crazy idea?
He forgot his notes so he had to **make up** his speech as he went along.

**d)** completing

The final chapter **sums up** all the arguments.
There are a couple of points we need to **clear up**.
They've decided to **wind up** their operations in Ireland and relocate.

**e)** going wrong

Don't **mix up** the dossiers or we'll never find the documents we need.
The office **slipped up** and the order was never sent.
The delay in the delivery of essential raw materials threatened to **hold up** production.

**Practice**

**A Multi-word verbs with *up***

Match the sentence halves.

| | | | |
|---|---|---|---|
| 1 | He may break up | **a)** | with what's been going on. |
| 2 | We need more facts to back up | **b)** | in conversation. |
| 3 | Her name often comes up | **c)** | it'll mess up all our plans. |
| 4 | I've been away so I need to catch up | **d)** | the terms of the contract. |
| 5 | If the bank refuses the loan | **e)** | under all the stress. |
| 6 | The lawyer has drawn up | **f)** | our arguments. |

**B Sentence completion**

Complete the sentences with these verbs.

| play up  follow up  pay up  work up  look up  face up to |
|---|

1 He's too young to .................. such a heavy responsibility.

2 The director will now .................. the committee's suggestions.

3 I just can't .................. any enthusiasm for the idea.

4 Now we have a new dynamic team, things will start to .................. .

5 Did the insurance company .................. after all that argument?

6 The mechanism has begun to .................. again and it needs an urgent repair.

**C Sentence completion**

Complete the sentences choosing from the following verbs. There are more verbs than necessary.

| think up  turn up  save up  clear up  set up  keep up  hold up  take up  do up |
|---|

1 How long did it take you to .................. for a new yacht?

2 Can you help me .................. this mess?

3 It's difficult to .................. with all the new developments.

4 He gave his son some capital to .................. his own business.

5 I don't want to .................. you .................. if you're in a hurry.

6 How did you .................. such a clever way out of the difficulty?

## Understanding multi-word verbs (2)

**2** *down*

**a)** reducing

The economy is overheating and needs to **slow down**.
We've started to explore ways of **keeping down** costs.
The government intends to **water down** its commitment to a clean air policy.

**b)** coming to an end

The shipyard is due to **close down** at the end of the year.
Mr Holzer has **stepped down** as vice-president.
Talks **broke down** before a deal could be reached.

**c)** writing / recording

I've **put** your name **down** on the list.
Could you please **write down** your name and address.
Make sure you **note down** every word she says.

**d)** defeating

Eventually, he had to **back down** and apologise.
The army quickly **put down** the rebellion.
Another series of public sector strikes could **bring** the government **down**.

**3** *over*

**a)** considering

Before I make any decision I'll need to **talk** it **over** with my boss.
Give me a couple of days to **think** it **over**.
Do you have a few minutes to **look over** what I've written?

**b)** changes

Eurotunnel will **hand over** 40% of its after-tax profits to the UK and French governments from 2050 onwards.
There has recently been a hostile attempt to **take over** our company.
Swiss banks yesterday gained a significant victory in their attempt to **win over** US public opinion.

## Practice

**A** Multi-word verbs with *down*

Complete the sentences with these verbs.

| play down | run down | break down | cut down | bring down | note down |
|---|---|---|---|---|---|

1 The talks are likely to ................... if both parties refuse a compromise.

2 The old system is being progressively ................... and will soon be replaced.

3 Retailers are having to ................... their prices to attract custom.

4 I'll just ................... your address and phone number.

5 In a time of rising costs we should ................... on our spending.

6 The minister is bound to ................... the scale of the disaster.

**B** Multi-word verbs with *up, down* and *over*

Match the sentence halves.

1 We've kept our prices down but, as a result,

2 They're winding up their operations in Brazil and

3 My father set up the company in 1982 and

4 The share price shot up 25%

5 The talks were on the point of breaking down

6 The prime minister stepped down when

7 Think it over and, if you agree to the terms,

a) I took over the business when he retired.

b) when we took over our nearest rival.

c) the São Paulo factory will close down soon.

d) we'll draw up a contract.

e) we've had to cut down on production costs.

f) she failed to win over public opinion.

g) when the Swedish ambassador came up with a brilliant solution.

## Understanding multi-word verbs (3)

**4** *off*

**a)** beginning

The emerging market of digital pay-TV is finally about to **take off**.

Repsol, the energy conglomerate, is likely to **spark off** a 'fat cat' controversy over director pay packets that could total Pta74.6 million.

The report **set off** a wave of early selling in the Treasury market.

**b)** stopping

The leader of the opposition said he was reluctant to **break off** talks with the government.

The crew of the damaged Mir space station were forced to **call off** a planned docking with a cargo ship after a computer failure.

They've decided to **put off** the meeting until next week.

**c)** reducing

Sales should **level off** now after reaching 375,000 units last year.

The novelty of frequent travel tends to **wear off** pretty quickly.

Interest rates have been raised to **cool off** inflationary pressures.

**5** *on*

continuing

Don't bother about me; just **carry on** with what you're doing.

The law suit **dragged on** and on for eight years.

Could you **hold on** for a few moments while I consult with my colleague?

**6** Verbs with two particles followed by an object

Examples include:

We need to **come up with** a solution soon. (= find / produce)

We should try to **cut down on** spending. (= reduce)

I'll **get on to** Mrs Butler and give you her reply shortly. (= contact)

It's difficult to **get on with** Mr Grundy; he's so bad-tempered. (= see eye to eye with)

It's vital to **keep up with** developments in information technology. (= be fully informed)

I **look forward to** seeing you again. (= anticipate with pleasure)

We're late so we'll have to work hard to **make up for** lost time. (= compensate for)

The failure can be **put down to** poor quality control. (= explained by / attributed to)

She wants more responsibility and has **put in for** promotion. (= applied for)

I've had to **put up with** a lot of unfair criticism. (= tolerate)

## Practice

### A Particles and their meaning

1 Match each particle (1–5) to one of the meanings (a–e).

| | | | |
|---|---|---|---|
| **1** up | | **a)** | writing / recording |
| **2** down | | **b)** | considering |
| **3** on | | **c)** | beginning |
| **4** off | | **d)** | continuing |
| **5** over | | **e)** | completing |

2 Combine the verbs below with a particle above to make a multi-word verb and then indicate its area of meaning.

**1** think *over = considering*　　**4** sum .......................　　**7** keep .......................

**2** spark .......................　　**5** look .......................

**3** wind .......................　　**6** note .......................

### B Sentence rearrangement

Put the words in order to make sentences.

**1** need we to for lost time make up

**2** back want to agreement out they of the

**3** the up firm strong against ran competition

**4** round after a drafting a to delay he long got reply

**5** a of have people put chairman's for the number job in

**6** thinks Roger he's an up with come problems answer our to

### C A phone conversation

Complete the following phone conversation using these verbs and particles.

```
call  fix  get  hold  put  read  tied
back  back  back  on  through  up  up
```

**A** Multiplex plc, can I help you?

**B** Yes, I'd like to speak to Mr Webster, please.

**A** Certainly, I'll just ................... you ...................[1]. Sorry, the line's busy. Would you like to ...................[2] or ...................[3] later?

**B** Um, could you take a message?

**A** Certainly.

**B** Could you tell him that I'll be ...................[4] all day Friday. So if he can ...................[5] to me we can ...................[6] another time to meet.

**A** Right, and your name?

**B** It's Kamal Ahmed on 020 7542 6688.

**A** I'll just ................... that ...................[7] to you. Kamal Ahmed on 020 7542 6688.

**B** Great. Thanks for your help.

# Adverbs

## Adverb position and uses (1)

**Form**
He **rarely** drinks alcohol.
I can **usually** take at least an hour for lunch.
She has **always** been devoted to the company.
She speaks Spanish **very well**.

From these examples we see that the adverb goes:

**a)** before the main verb
**b)** between a modal (e.g. *could*, *will*) and the main verb
**c)** between two auxiliaries for frequency adverbs
**d)** after the direct object (NOT *She speaks very well Spanish.)

The adverb comes after the verb *to be*:

I am **still** waiting.
She was **obviously** delighted.
We are **always** ready to pay you a visit.

**Uses**

**1** Saying how, where, when, how often something happens or is done

He went
**quickly / by train / alone**.
**there / home / up to the second floor**.
**recently / a couple of weeks ago**.

**2** Modifying verbs and adjectives

Prices have gone up **excessively**.
Microchips are **very** cheap.
She **almost** forgot to take her passport.
She is **terribly** forgetful.

His idea is **completely** out of the question.
She is **absolutely** fabulous.
They **totally** disagree with our position.
It's been **remarkably** successful.

**3** Describing the rate of change

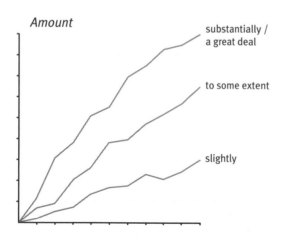

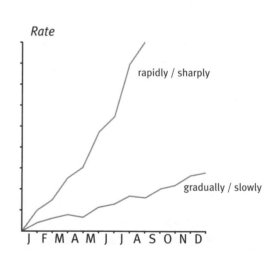

**Practice**

### A Sentence rearrangement

The words in the following sentences are in the wrong order. Rewrite them in the correct order.

1 For confirmation I still am waiting.

2 I wear never jeans at work.

3 He speaks very well Greek.

4 Cheaper I will be probably able to get it.

5 To welcome visitors I always am pleased.

6 Her idea completely is absurd.

### B Adverb position

Complete this e-mail by placing the adverbs in the correct position on each line.

| | |
|---|---|
| Hi! Thanks for your last e-mail. I'm sorry I haven't | very |
| got back to you sooner but we've been rushed | terribly |
| in the office. We seem to be so busy. | always |
| It seems the launch has been successful, | remarkably |
| beyond our wildest dreams in fact. We are delighted | obviously |
| and we have had a large order from a company | already |
| in China. This is fabulous news. See you soon. | absolutely |

### C Describing the rate of change

How would you describe the sales growth of the items below?

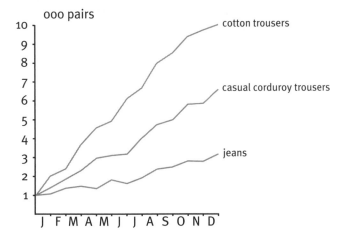

000 pairs

cotton trousers

casual corduroy trousers

jeans

J F M A M J J A S O N D

## Adverb position and uses (2)

**4 Changing focus and emphasis**

The position of adverbs in a sentence is often flexible. This enables the speaker to make changes of focus and emphasis. The following are the *common* positions according to their function. For reasons of emphasis these positions may on occasion be different.

**a)** at the beginning of the sentence

| | |
|---|---|
| OPINION | **In actual fact** I think she's wrong.<br>**Hopefully** the situation will get better.<br>**Fortunately** the damage was slight. |
| TIME | **A year ago** they decided to go public.<br>**To date** we have received 321 requests for information.<br>**Originally** the firm used to produce horseshoes. |

**b)** in the middle of the sentence

| | |
|---|---|
| MANNER | Prices could **suddenly** rise. |
| FREQUENCY | They **never** pay on time.<br>I **occasionally** read *The Economist*. |
| OPINION | Her work record is **quite honestly** awful. |
| TIME | I am **still** waiting for permission.<br>We have **already** sold over 50,000 units.<br>Have you **ever** been to Finland? |

**c)** at the end of the sentence

| | |
|---|---|
| MANNER | I think the presentation went **well.**<br>He works **fast.** |
| PLACE | She has never been **there.**<br>You'll find him working **downstairs.** |
| TIME | The board talked about the share flotation **yesterday.**<br>We'll have the prototype ready **soon.**<br>I haven't seen Mr Khomsi **lately.** |

**5 Order**

If there are a number of adverbs in the same sentence the order is usually:

**1)** Manner    **2)** Place    **3)** Time

We went to Madrid last month. (NOT *last month to Madrid)
They negotiated aggressively for four hours. (NOT *for four hours aggressively)

## Practice

### A Commenting on the situation

Match the sentences in column A with those in column B.

**A**

1 It was his first real job interview for three years.
2 He missed the bus and thought he would be late.
3 During the interview they asked him why he wanted to work for their firm.
4 They said 'Don't contact us, we'll contact you'.
5 He then did a course on interview skills.
6 He got to know a lot of famous musicians and went on tour with them.

**B**

a) **Eventually** he set up his own label and became a millionaire.
b) **Shortly after** he managed to find a job with a major record label.
c) **Luckily** someone gave him a lift and he got there on time.
d) **Naturally** he felt very nervous.
e) **Foolishly** he said that he just needed the money and any job would do.
f) **Obviously** he hadn't got the job.

### B Your situation

Using an appropriate adverb, respond to these questions about your own work situation, as in the example.

Example:

How quickly do your colleagues work?

*They work extremely fast.*

1 Do they ever arrive late for work?
2 Where do you usually work?
3 How well do you get on with your boss?
4 Have you seen him or her recently?
5 What do you think of his / her performance? (be honest)

### C Adverb position

Insert the adverbs into each line of this message in the most natural position.

| | |
|---|---|
| Thank you for the e-mail you sent. I have spoken to Eric | yesterday; already |
| but he says he is waiting for confirmation from the board | still |
| before we can go ahead with the proposed changes. The delay | quite frankly |
| is getting on my nerves but I hope to get started on the project. | very soon |
| As is the case, we will receive confirmation at the last | often; suddenly |
| minute and have to work for the next couple of months | flat out |
| in order to get into production. | fast |

# Nouns
# (identifying people and things)

## Noun formation

We use some words only as nouns: *car, cupboard, biscuit*, etc. In other cases, nouns can be derived from other words, notably from verbs by adding a suffix. For example:

deliver → deliver**y**    employ → employ**ment**    exhibit → exhibi**tion**

Some of the common noun endings are:

depart → depart**ure**    initiate → initia**tive**    perform → perform**ance**    promote → promo**tion**
recruit → recruit**ment**    refer → refer**ence**    store → stor**age**    train → train**ing**

Nouns can also be formed from adjectives or other nouns:

accurate → accura**cy**    capital → capital**ism**    effective → effective**ness**    free → free**dom**
partner → partner**ship**    reliable → reliabi**lity**

Some nouns have the same form as verbs. For example:

attempt   benefit   blame   budget   call   claim   copy   cost   delay
help   lack   offer   share   supply   support   try   wait   walk   wish

Sometimes the pronunciation is different, even though the noun and the verb have the same form:

| Verb | Noun | Verb | Noun |
|------|------|------|------|
| con'duct | 'conduct | pro'duce | 'produce |
| dis'count | 'discount | re'cord | 'record |
| im'port | 'import | re'ject | 'reject |
| ob'ject | 'object | sub'ject | 'subject |
| per'mit | 'permit | trans'fer | 'transfer |

### Activities

A frequent way of forming nouns is by adding *-ing* to a verb. In this way, we can refer to an action, activity or process in a general way. The noun or noun phrase may be the subject or the object of the verb:

**Training** is essential for a flexible labour force.
She has to do a lot of **entertaining**.
**Making money** is not everything in life.
More has to be done to prevent **counterfeiting**.

### People

Nouns referring to people can be formed with *-er, -or, -ian, -ee, -ant* and *-ist*:

lawy**er**   act**or**   technic**ian**   train**ee**   consult**ant**   dent**ist**
report**er**   audit**or**   music**ian**   employ**ee**   assist**ant**   scient**ist**

## Practice

**A** Noun formation

Using a dictionary if necessary, complete the two columns with nouns derived from the verbs and adjectives given. Use the suffixes on the opposite page.

| Verb | Noun | Adjective | Noun |
|------|------|-----------|------|
| accept | .................. | wise | .................. |
| agree | .................. | weak | .................. |
| counterfeit | .................. | reliable | .................. |
| enter (2 answers) | .................. | prosperous | .................. |
| initiate | .................. | social (2 answers) | .................. |
| occur | .................. | punctual | .................. |
| protect | .................. | real | .................. |
| race (2 answers) | .................. | complex | .................. |
| refer | .................. | effective | .................. |
| store | .................. | aware | .................. |
| waste | .................. | creative (2 answers) | .................. |

**B** Activities

Match the sentence halves.

1 Flying on a charter flight
2 Reducing poverty and homelessness
3 Making a profit for the shareholders
4 Speaking in front of a large audience
5 Setting up a joint venture abroad
6 Headhunting

**a)** is the primary aim of most businesses.
**b)** is a way of breaking into an export market.
**c)** is a priority for the new left-wing government.
**d)** is an effective method of recruiting key executives.
**e)** can be a stressful experience.
**f)** is cheaper than on a scheduled one.

**C** People

Complete each sentence with a noun that refers to the type of person described.

1 He works at the reception desk so he's a .................. .
2 A contract is signed by both the employer and the .................. .
3 He works in the legal department so he's a .................. .
4 As an .................. she audits the company's accounts.
5 She plays a musical instrument so she's a .................. .
6 She studied electricity and became an .................. .
7 As a .................. for the *Financial Times* he reports on events around the world.
8 As a freelance .................. he can sell his photos to newspapers and magazines.
9 Over 200 people applied for the job we advertised; we didn't expect so many .................. .

## Types of noun

Nouns belong to two broad families: *countable nouns* and *uncountable nouns*.

*Countable* nouns include:

- individual things, people and places:
  a diary, a memo, a photo, a receptionist, a factory, a corridor
- units of measurement:
  a metre, a mile, a kilo, a pound, a litre, a gallon

*Countable* nouns:

- are used with *a / an*
- can be used in the plural (*diaries, memos,* etc.)
- follow words such as *many, these, those, several, few, a few, a number of*

*Uncountable* nouns include:

- substances:
  gas, glass, gold, iron, oil, plastic, water, etc.
- many abstract ideas:
  access, freedom, health, humour, profitability, progress, relevance, safety, etc.
- verbal nouns:
  brainstorming, job-sharing, restructuring, shopping, timing

*Uncountable* nouns:

- do not take *the* when used in a general sense (NOT *the travel broadens the mind)
- take the singular form of the verb
- have words like *much, little, a little, some, a great deal of* before them

Some of the more common uncountable nouns are:

accommodation  advertising  advice  baggage  brainstorming  cash
clothing  damage  employment  equipment  furniture  hardware  information
insurance  legislation  merchandise  money  news  progress  research
software  traffic  training  transport  travel  weather  work

It is possible to refer to one example of an uncountable noun by using a countable expression before it or by using another word or expression:

accommodation: a place to live
advice: a piece of advice
information: a piece of information
insurance: an insurance policy
money: a coin / a banknote / a sum
progress: a step forward
training: a training course
work: a job / task

## Practice

**A** Countable or uncountable?

Decide whether the following nouns are used as countable nouns or uncountable nouns, as in the examples.

She has had three years' **experience** as a solicitor. ..*U*..

The demotion was a painful **experience**. ..*C*..

1 Are you here for **business** or pleasure? ......

2 He has set up a small fashion **business**. ......

3 I've never read the **works** of Shakespeare. ......

4 She's found **work** as a commercial assistant. ......

5 Have you got a **light**? ......

6 Were you able to throw any **light** on the subject? ......

7 We'll need some more wine **glasses** for the reception. ......

8 Fifty per cent of our bottles are made of recycled **glass**. ......

9 They failed to reach an **agreement**. ......

10 Is there **agreement** on how much will be spent? ......

11 Self-**advertisement** is not always a good thing. ......

12 We put an **advertisement** in the *Financial Times*. ......

**B** Matching countable and uncountable nouns

Match each countable noun with an uncountable noun with a similar meaning.

traffic   equipment   insurance   machines   accidents   cars   employment   policies
travel   advice   news   laws   legislation   damage   jobs   journey   bulletins   hints

| Countable | Uncountable |
|---|---|
| ............................. | ............................. |
| ............................. | ............................. |
| ............................. | ............................. |
| ............................. | ............................. |
| ............................. | ............................. |
| ............................. | ............................. |
| ............................. | ............................. |
| ............................. | ............................. |
| ............................. | ............................. |

## Plural nouns

We add -*s* to form the plural of most nouns. If the noun ends in -*s*, -*x*, -*ch* or -*sh*, we add -*es*:

class**es**   box**es**   church**es**   crash**es**

We also add -*es* to the following:

hero → hero**es**   potato → potato**es**   tomato → tomato**es**

If the final consonant of a noun is followed by -*y*, it is changed into -*ies*:

delivery → deliver**ies**   party → part**ies**   worry → worr**ies**

There are nouns which only occur in the plural. For example:

**Earnings** per share have increased.
Their **headquarters** are in Boston.
The **goods** will be sent by special delivery.
Don't leave **valuables** in your car.
I'm getting fat and my **trousers** are too tight.
All her **clothes** were lost at the airport.
We've opened new **premises** in Warsaw.
**Refreshments** are available in the lobby.
He lives on the **outskirts** of the town.
Many **thanks** for your invitation.
What **means** of transport do you prefer?
**Works** Entrance

### Singular nouns ending in -*s*

Some nouns end in -*s* but are not plural:

The news **was** good.
Politics **has** never been one of my favourite subjects.
Economics **is** not an exact science.
Rabies **is** a dangerous disease.

### Irregular plurals

Some words do not take an -*s* but have other forms, other endings or stay the same:

aircraft → aircraft   criterion → criteria   foot → feet   formula → formulae (or formulas)
half → halves   life → lives   matrix → matrices   person → people   phenomenon → phenomena
tooth → teeth   woman → women

### Groups and organisations

Singular nouns such as *bank* or *committee* can be seen either as a number of people (plural) or as a collective unit (singular). As a result, the following verb or pronoun may be either singular or plural.

The bank **has** sent me my new credit card.
The committee **have** shelved the project.

Other words in this category include:

club   firm   government   management   media   police   public   staff   team   union

**Practice**

**A Nouns only occurring in the plural**

Complete the sentences using these words.

| refreshments premises valuables goods works crossroads outskirts means |
|---|

1 Their offices are on the .................. of Milan.
2 The money was acquired by dishonest .................. .
3 Please hand in all .................. at the reception desk.
4 The demand for .................. and services is lower this year.
5 Our new .................. are located downtown near the municipal library.
6 He's the official in charge of the engineering .................. .
7 ..................: tea, coffee and snacks, will be served during the break.
8 When I became redundant for the first time I felt I had reached a .................. in my life.

**B Making nouns plural**

What is the plural of the following words?

1 bag          6 shelf
2 person       7 fax
3 party        8 knife
4 formula      9 criterion
5 potato       10 match

**C Singular or plural?**

Complete the sentences with *is*, *are*, *has* or *have*.

1 Statistics .................. a subject about which I know very little.
2 The goods you ordered .................. arrived.
3 All their belongings .................. in their hotel room.
4 People .................. often strange.
5 Mathematics .................. often used as a test of intelligence.
6 The government .................. brought in a new piece of legislation.

**D Common mistakes**

Correct the errors in these sentences.

1 The news are bad, I'm afraid.
2 She knows a great many persons.
3 Stress at work is not a recent phenomena.
4 Our office is situated in a pleasant surrounding.
5 The staffs are unhappy with the new arrangements.

## Two nouns together

There are three main ways of putting two nouns together:

**1** *noun + 's + noun*

the president's decision
the agent's fee

**2** *noun + preposition + noun*

the punishment of fraud
an article on the theatre

**3** *compound nouns*

a market survey
consumer confidence

### 1 Noun + 's + noun

We use the *'s* structure to express the relationships between nouns:

| | |
|---|---|
| possession | John's briefcase, Mr Smith's office |
| relationships | my wife's name, his brother's success |
| duration and time | a month's holiday, yesterday's papers, this year's results |

*'s* can be used to show that something belongs to or is associated with a place or an organisation:

| | | |
|---|---|---|
| New York's Fifth Avenue | Amsterdam's canals | Moscow's Red Square |
| the board's decision | the company's profits | the bank's important clients |

*'s* is added to a noun that specifies a part of an object or a quality it has:

| | | |
|---|---|---|
| the car's design | the computer's memory | the plane's wing |

### 2 Noun + *of* + noun

When we want to talk about a particular unit of something, we use a countable noun before an uncountable noun linked by *of*. For example:

| | | | |
|---|---|---|---|
| a piece of equipment | an item of news | a piece of paper | a piece of software |
| a bit of land | a bit of trouble | a bit of research | a run of bad luck |

Some constructions are relatively fixed combinations:

| | | |
|---|---|---|
| a word of advice | a show of strength | a spell of bad weather |
| a mountain of work | a round of talks / negotiations | a stroke of luck |

Expressions of measurement follow this pattern:

| | | |
|---|---|---|
| a gallon of petrol | a pint of beer | a kilo of rice |

The *of* structure is used to refer to containers and their contents. The noun + noun structure refers to the container without its contents:

| | |
|---|---|
| a barrel of oil | an oil barrel |
| a packet of cigarettes | a cigarette packet |
| a jar of coffee | a coffee jar |
| a glass of wine | a wine glass |

We also use an *of* structure with words that indicate a part of something:

| | |
|---|---|
| the middle of the meeting | the bottom of the page |
| the back of the building | the end of my stay |

## Practice

**A Famous places**

Match the place name and the feature it is famous for.

> ~~Copenhagen~~  Berlin  canals  Madrid  London  Venice  ~~mermaid~~  New York
> Cairo  skyscrapers  Prado  Brandenburg Gate  pyramids  Big Ben

Example: *Copenhagen's mermaid.*

**B Quantities**

Match an expression on the left with the appropriate noun on the right.

| | |
|---|---|
| a lump of | coffee |
| a can of | salt |
| a jar of | beer |
| a bar of | milk |
| a carton of | chocolate |
| a grain of | sugar |

**C Noun + *of* + noun**

Study the entries from the *Longman Business English Dictionary* and complete the sentences below.

*...fund, the lower the net return to investors.*
**rate of return** plural **rates of return** [C] the amount of profit that a particular investment will make, expressed as a percentage: *Merrill Lynch Ready Assets Trust showed an annual rate of return of 5.42%.*

*...which sought protection from creditors...y in the year.*
**basket of currencies** *n* plural **baskets of currencies** [C usually singular] a group of currencies against which the value of another currency is measured: *The yen's exchange rate against a basket of currencies has fallen to its lowest level for three months.*—see also MARKET BASKET

*Breach of confidence.*
**breach of contract** *n* plural **breaches of contract** [C,U] LAW when someone fails to do something that they have agreed to do in a contract: *Watson had to pay more than £55 million in damages for breach of contract.* | *Their tactic was to say that all striking drivers were **in breach of contract**, and fire them.*

*...indebtness to banks and others.*
**letter of credit** written abbreviation **l/c** *n* plural **letters of credit** [C] **1** in foreign trade, a written promise by an importer's bank to pay the exporter's bank on a particular date or at a particular time after the goods are sent by the exporter: *Coffee buyers in Central America are required to have proof of financing, such as a letter of credit.*

*...by manufacturers.*
**conflict of interest** *n* plural **conflicts of interest** [C,U] a situation in which you cannot do your job fairly because you have the power to decide something in a way that would be to your advantage, although this may not be the best decision: *There is a growing conflict of interest between her position as a politician and her business activities.*

1  The value of the yen against a selected .................... has fallen to 85% of its 1999 value.
2  Her refusal to work flexible hours constituted a .................... .
3  We would expect a .................... of at least 15% on our investment.
4  Being both a member of parliament and CEO of a major firm could lead to a .................... .
5  The bank has opened a confirmed an irrevocable .................... in your favour.

## Compound nouns

### 1 Nouns used as adjectives

In the noun + noun structure, the first noun functions like an adjective and describes the second noun. Very often, the first noun answers the question *What kind?*

a bank transfer (a kind of transfer)
work experience (a type of experience)
a bank loan (a kind of loan)
a work permit (a type of permit)

We can also make compound nouns when the first noun ends in *-ing*:

the training budget    a spending review    a turning point

### 2 Singular with a plural meaning

In a compound noun the first noun is usually singular, even if it has a plural meaning:

a record store (a store that sells records)
a cheque book (a book containing cheques)
a car factory (a factory that produces cars)

Nouns in numerical expression are always singular:

a four-star hotel    a five-year plan    a 35-hour week
a 50-dollar bill    a 10-ton truck    a million-dollar loan

However, the *s* is kept on the first noun in the following expressions:

accounts department    clothes store    customs officer    futures market
goods train    incomes policy    needs analysis    overseas branch
savings account    sports car    sales policy    works manager

### 3 Choice of structures

Sometimes only one construction is possible:

a breach of contract (NOT *a contract's breach, a breach contract)
the terms of reference (NOT *reference terms, terms' reference)
Peter's friends (NOT *the friends of Peter, Peter friends)
a traffic jam (NOT *a traffic's jam, a jam's traffic, the traffic of jam)
a silicon chip (NOT *a silicon's chip, a chip's silicon, a chip of silicon)

Sometimes it is possible to use two structures but it is not possible to use all three:

the decision of the board    the board's decision (NOT *the board decision)
the responsibilities of the project manager    the project manager's responsibilities (NOT *the project manager responsibilities)

## Practice

**A  Noun combinations**

One word can be used each time to make compound nouns, as in the example.

Example:

answer ...*phone*......          ......*phone*...... card          ...*phone*...... number

1  .................. pitch          .................. figures          .................. hype

2  savings ..................          bank ..................          .................. number

3  bear ..................          .................. leader          home ..................

4  .................. awareness          .................. image          .................. loyalty

5  .................. concessions          .................. secret          .................. union

**B  Choice of structures**

Put a tick (✓) if the expression is correct and a cross (✗) if it is incorrect, as in the examples.

Examples:

a point of view  ✓

a viewpoint  ✓

a view's point  ✗

| | | |
|---|---|---|
| 1 a window of opportunity | 7 data collection | 13 a spending's review |
| 2 an opportunity's window | 8 data's collection | 14 an eight-hour day |
| 3 a promise's breach | 9 a savings account | 15 an eight hours day |
| 4 a breach of promise | 10 a saving account | 16 an eight hours' day |
| 5 a sales target | 11 a spending review | 17 a plant of recycling |
| 6 a target of sales | 12 a review of spending | 18 a recycling plant |

**C  Compound nouns**

Use these words to make compound to fill in the blanks.

| figures   sense   loyalty   revenue   production   ~~operas~~ |
|---|

Soap.....*operas*..... are the economic powerhouses of television ..................[1]. They are cheap to make and enjoy high viewing ..................[2]. And the income is secure. They tend to run forever and the stars are not paid a lot for the time they spend on screen. They make good business ..................[3] for broadcasters for they act as a focal point for the audience, building up viewer ..................[4] and attracting advertising ..................[5].

## Nouns and prepositions

It can be difficult to know what preposition comes after a noun.

> The insurance industry last week published a code of practice on genetics. It says companies will seek medical **advice on** how to interpret tests.

> Internal reorganisation was cited as the main **reason for** redundancies by 49.8% of the organisations surveyed.

> The English do not put the same resources into language teaching as others, and since the 17th century there has never been any particular **interest in** foreign languages.

Here is a list of nouns and the prepositions that follow them:

| | | |
|---|---|---|
| the alternative **to** job cuts | interest **in** my idea | a rise **in** prices |
| attention **to** detail | a need **for** change | a rise **of** 5% |
| an application **for** a grant | an order **for** goods | the solution **to** the problem |
| a cheque **for** £2,000 | the reason **for** the change | a tax **on** cigarettes |
| value **for** money | a request **for** more time | fall **in** demand |
| a fall **of** 3% | the return **on** investment | a vote **of** confidence |

### Prepositional phrases

Prepositional phrases are formed when a noun follows a preposition. All the phrases below are common:

**at:** your disposal   our expense   a profit/loss   your risk   short notice

**beyond:** our control   reasonable doubt   our wildest dreams

**by:** accident   law   mistake

**in:** advance   arrears   bulk   demand   debt   force   due course   full   good condition   stock   transit

**on:** approval   arrival   closer inspection   delivery   display   loan   a regular basis   request   sale   schedule

**out of:** date   order   stock   work

**through:** the usual channels   no fault of our own

**under:** pressure   separate cover   way

**within:** a week   the next few months

**Practice**

**A** **Which preposition?**

Complete the sentences with a suitable preposition.

**1** Thank you for your interest ................... our proposal.

**2** There has been a fall ................... demand for their products.

**3** There has been a fall ................... 2.5% in the volume of sales.

**4** What was the reason ................... his resignation?

**5** The government is increasing the tax ................... cigarettes.

**6** I made out a cheque ................... 300 euros.

**7** She is meticulous and pays great attention ................... detail.

**8** Plans are ................... way for a new link road.

**B** **Prepositional phrases**

Which preposition completes each set of three sentences?

**1**

The error was due to circumstances ................... our control.

It started off good-humouredly but then went ................... a joke.

Roger Penrose is, ................... a doubt, one of the great minds of our time.

**2**

................... law, you have to carry an identity card in many countries.

I met her quite ................... chance in the street in Munich.

Someone left the door open ................... mistake.

**3**

I will be in touch ................... due course.

We're ................... luck; there's still one left.

The debt must be paid ................... full by 31 January.

**4**

Mr Evans will meet you ................... your arrival.

I don't always use the car; I try to go ................... foot whenever possible.

The goods seemed all right but ................... closer inspection at least 30% were defective.

**5**

Mrs Gonzales cannot see you ................... such short notice.

A chauffeur-driven car will be put ................... your disposal.

I attended the reception ................... the chairman's invitation.

# UNIT 12 | Identifying nouns

## Articles (*a* / *an*, *the* and zero article)

**Form**  We use *a* when the next word begins with a consonant sound and *an* when it begins with a vowel sound:

> a bill   a European   a house   a magazine   a union   an ability
> an estimate   an hour   an MBA   an umbrella

### Uses of *a* / *an*, *the* and zero article (Ø)

1  Before unspecified singular countable nouns:

   He lives in **a** flat. (we don't know anything else about it)

2  Before professions:

   She's **a** chemical engineer and he's **a** project manager.

3  In expressions of measurement:

   The speed limit is 55 miles **an** hour.
   It costs €1.15 **a** litre.

4  To describe 'all examples of the same kind':

   **A** balance sheet is **a** document that lists assets and liabilities.

5  Before a specific noun that we have mentioned before:

   I had a Jaguar and a Mercedes but I sold **the** Jaguar to my brother.

6  When it is clear what particular thing or place is meant:

   I'll meet you in **the** staff car park behind **the** warehouse.    Where are **the** toilets?

7  When two nouns are joined with *of*:

   **the** history **of** commerce   **the** balance **of** trade   **a** mountain **of** photocopying   **a** breach **of** contract

8  Before adjectives to specify a category of people or things:

   **the** rich   **the** poor   **the** middle classes   **the** mobile phone (a type of phone)   **the** textile industry

9  Before some institutions:

   **the** United Nations   **the** IMF   **the** Bundesbank   **the** BBC

10  In superlative expressions:

   General Motors is **the** biggest car manufacturer.

11  With uncountable nouns used in a general sense:

   Nothing succeeds like **(Ø)** success.    **(Ø)** Information is **(Ø)** power.
   **(Ø)** Unity is **(Ø)** strength.

12  Before unspecified plural nouns:

   **(Ø)** People often distrust **(Ø)** politicians.

13  Before the names of places and people:
   **(Ø)** Oxford   **(Ø)** Singapore   **(Ø)** Dr Schweitzer   **(Ø)** President Lincoln

## Practice

### A  *a / an*, *the* and zero article

Read the following passage and identify the uses of *a / an*, *the* and zero article with each noun. Give them a number which corresponds to one of the categories on the previous page (1–13).

My brother Michael used to be a teacher ..*Category 2*..¹ in a village school ..*Category 1*...² near Cambridge ....................³. The job ....................⁴ was interesting but tiring and not very well-paid. He spent most of his free time on his hobby – collecting and repairing antique clocks ....................⁵. Then he had an idea ....................⁶. The CBI ....................⁷ (Confederation of British Industry) was helping people ....................⁸ start up by themselves. Why not go on a training course ....................⁹, apply for a loan ....................¹⁰ and set up a small business ....................¹¹?

So he sent in his resignation to the school ....................¹², said goodbye to the children ....................¹³, and joined the unemployed ....................¹⁴. He obtained information ....................¹⁵ from different sources ....................¹⁶, took advice ....................¹⁷ from an accountant ....................¹⁸, left the village ....................¹⁹ and learnt all about the antique trade ....................²⁰. Eighteen months later he had his own shop and was earning about £2,000 a month ....................²¹. 'It was the best thing ....................²² I ever did,' he says.

### B  Ferrari

Complete the blanks with *a / an*, *the* or Ø.

........*Ø*.......... Enzo Ferrari's death in August 1988 was ....................¹ sad occasion. However, it did release ....................² Ferrari from ....................³ grip of his idiosyncratic ways and enabled ....................⁴ firm to move into ....................⁵ new era.

....................⁶ appointment of Luca di Montezemolo in December 1991 was ....................⁷ beginning of ....................⁸ series of ....................⁹ changes. His aim was to invest in ....................¹⁰ research and ....................¹¹ development and to bridge ....................¹² gap between ....................¹³ racing and production car businesses. He also introduced ....................¹⁴ sponsorship, although ....................¹⁵ constructor still has fewer names on its cars than ....................¹⁶ other teams. ....................¹⁷ CEO is steering ....................¹⁸ narrow course between modernising ....................¹⁹ company while trying to avoid diluting ....................²⁰ mystique that makes ....................²¹ marque so great.

*Enzo Ferrari*

*Luca di Montezemolo*

## Quantifiers (1)

**1 Talking about unspecific amounts**

We use *some* with both plural countable nouns or uncountable nouns to talk about a quantity or number without being very precise:

**Some** people are workaholics.
Operating profits were **some** £180 million.
Would you like **some** coffee?
**Some** analysts are saying that the crisis will continue for **some** time.

We use *any* most commonly in negative sentences and in questions to talk about a quantity of something that may or may not exist:

Have you **any** baggage with you?
There isn't **any** time left.
We haven't got **any** components in stock.
Do you have **any** tickets for the concert?

**2 Talking about total amounts**

*Any* can indicate that *all* examples of the noun are to be included:

**Any** manager will tell you that good organisation is important. (= all managers)
An e-mail can be received at **any** time of the day or night. (= 24 hours a day)
Choose **any** model you like. (= it doesn't matter which model)

*All* and *all of* are both possible before a noun with a determiner:

He's taken **all** (**of**) the paper.

If there is no determiner we do not use *of* with a plural countable noun:

**All** formal meetings are a waste of time in his opinion. (NOT *all of meetings)

Note that *all* does not go between *the* and a noun:

He spent the **whole** meeting looking at his watch. (NOT *the all meeting)

**3 Zero quantities**

*No* and *none of* mean 'not any' and 'not one':

We've had **no** complaints about our services. (= we have not received any)
They have paid **none of** their invoices. (= not one)
**None** of the initial ideas **was** accepted. (note the singular verb form)

**Practice**

**A Amounts**

Complete the sentences using *some*, *any*, *no* or *none*.

1 We haven't had ................... news from our agent.

2 I have absolutely ................... idea what he wants.

3 The deal was worth ................... $16 billion.

4 ................... of his proposals were very good.

5 ................... of his proposals was very good.

6 He has ................... very old bottles of wine in his cellar.

7 We employ people of ................... race, religion or ethnic origin.

8 There is ................... point in wasting ................... more time on this issue.

9 I am enclosing ................... information about our range of products.

10 'Have you got ................... extra leaflets?' 'Sorry, there are ................... left.'

11 My new car uses hardly ................... petrol at all compared to my previous one.

12 ................... ill-advised people try to get by in Japan without hiring a good interpreter.

**B A letter of complaint**

Complete this letter using *all*, *some*, *any*, *no* or *none*.

Dear Mr Andrews,

I am sending this letter by registered mail as ...................[1] of my previous correspondence has received a reply.

You will recall from our agreement of Jan 3 this year that ...................[2] delay in the delivery of essential components would be subject to a penalty clause. So far we have received ...................[3] word from your plant manager that the components we ordered ...................[4] three weeks ago have been sent.

I would be grateful if you would take ...................[5] the necessary steps to ensure that these components are received without ...................[6] further delay otherwise we will have ...................[7] option but to enforce the penalty clause in the contract.

Yours sincerely,

*Proverb*

You can fool all people some of the time and some people all of the time, but you can't fool all people all of the time.

## Quantifiers (2)

### 4 Referring to large amounts

*Much* and *many* mean a large quantity or number of something. *Much* is used with uncountable nouns and *many* with countable ones:

**Many** decisions are made without **much** thought.
Did you meet **many** people at the conference?
We haven't made **much** progress recently.
How **much** money do you want to earn?

Both *many* and *much* can be replaced by *a lot of*. *Many* can be replaced by *a large number* (*of*) and *much* by *a great deal of*:

We stock **many / a large number of** spare parts in the warehouse.
We've spent **a great deal of** time on this project.

Note that we avoid using *much* in positive statements:

The fire did **a lot of** damage. (NOT *much damage)

### 5 Talking about limited amounts

*A few* and *some* are used with countable nouns to refer to a restricted quantity:

I like **a few / some** Australian wines but not all of them.
I've got **a few** minutes to spare.

*A little* and *some* are used with uncountable nouns:

I've got **a little / some** cash on me, but not much.

*A little* can be used with adjectives to mean 'to a certain extent':

The size of the deficit was **a little** surprising.

*A little* and *a few* point in a positive direction; *little* and *few* are more negative:

He has (very) **little** initiative and always waits to be told what to do.
There is **little** we can do about it, we'll just have to wait and see.
**Few** employees enjoy being appraised.
(Very) **few** people read philosophy for pleasure.

### 6 Talking about excessive / insufficient amounts

We use *too* before adjectives and adverbs, and before *much, many, few* and *little*. We use *enough* after adjectives and adverbs, and before nouns.

She drives **too** fast. I'm scared when I'm in a car with her.
I've never been trekking – it's probably **too** tiring and I'm **not** fit **enough**.
I haven't got **enough** money to buy a helicopter.
He didn't react quickly **enough**.

**Practice**

**A  Correct the errors**

All the following sentences are grammatically incorrect. Rewrite them correctly.

 1  He didn't reply enough fast.

 2  The flood caused many damage.

 3  What she said was a few strange.

 4  The whole process uses very few electricity.

 5  I enjoyed few of her books, but not all of them.

 6  We haven't made many progress recently.

 7  I don't think he has experience enough for the job.

 8  She works mostly on her own so she has very little colleagues.

 9  I've got few minutes to spare so we can continue if you like.

10  The final date for submission was three weeks ago so it's far very late now.

**B  A memo**

Complete the following memo using these words. You will need to use one word twice and one blank has two possible answers.

| little   few   much   too   a great deal of   a little   a few   many   enough |
|---|

## MEMO

FROM:   LC

TO:   Malcolm Bridgewater

Date:   May 4th

Subject:  Sales and promotion

Sales figures for the year to date have been ..................[1] disappointing as ..................[2] distributors are willing to promote our products as ..................[3] as we would like. The commission is relatively low and therefore there is very ..................[4] incentive for them to ensure volume sales. This said, sales of some lines have done better in the run-up to Christmas.

We recently did a survey of 1,500 customers. Unfortunately, very ..................[5] of those questioned (7%) said that our designs were attractive and ..................[6] people (over half of the respondents) felt they were ..................[7] old-fashioned. As a result I have commissioned a new design and spent ..................[8] time with the marketing department. I am sending you ..................[9] samples for you to comment on and, if you have ..................[10] time between now and the New Year, I'd be grateful for your comments.

# Describing nouns

## Adjectives

**Form** Many adjectives are not derived from other words:

old   new   high   low   rich   poor   hard   soft

However, you can recognise many adjectives from their endings. The word the adjective is derived from is either a noun or a verb. Here is a list of the most common endings, together with nouns that the adjectives often combine with:

| | | |
|---|---|---|
| **-able:** adjustable seatbelt | profitable venture | workable arrangement |
| **-al:** professional image | international dimension | promotional literature |
| **-ant:** important decision | pleasant meal | dominant partner |
| **-ary:** monetary policy | supplementary benefit | voluntary redundancy |
| **-ed:** limited company | satisfied customer | vested interest |
| **-ent:** confident manner | convenient time | independent survey |
| **-ful:** successful career | careful planning | fruitful discussion |
| **-ial:** industrial sabotage | judicial enquiry | potential disaster |
| **-ible:** deductible income | legible handwriting | negligible amount |
| **-ic:** economic policy | realistic forecast | strategic acquisition |
| **-ing:** convincing argument | leading brand | boring meeting |
| **-ive:** competitive salary | exclusive distributor | positive outlook |
| **-less:** endless discussion | hopeless case | useless idea |
| **-ly:** costly mistake | quarterly statement | timely intervention |
| **-ous:** ambitious politician | famous actor | tremendous increase |
| **-y:** busy employee | risky venture | wealthy banker |

### Forming opposites

Very often we use prefixes such as *dis-*, *il-*, *im-*, *in-*, *ir-*, *mis-* and *un-* to create negative forms of adjectives:

| | | |
|---|---|---|
| dishonest | disorganised | dissatisfied |
| illegal | illegible | illicit |
| impatient | impossible | impractical |
| inaccurate | incompetent | informal |
| irregular | irrevocable | irrecoverable |
| mismanaged | misinformed | mistaken |
| uneconomic | unfashionable | unsuccessful |

**Practice**

**A Your personal profile**

The personal profile grid can help you reveal your personality! Place a tick (✓) in the boxes next to the five words that describe you best. Put a cross (✗) next to the five words that are least applicable to you.

| | | | | | | | |
|---|---|---|---|---|---|---|---|
| persuasive | ☐ | original | ☐ | dutiful | ☐ | pleasant | ☐ |
| cheerful | ☐ | loyal | ☐ | courageous | ☐ | happy | ☐ |
| competitive | ☐ | sociable | ☐ | considerate | ☐ | playful | ☐ |
| submissive | ☐ | inspiring | ☐ | adventurous | ☐ | talkative | ☐ |
| conventional | ☐ | decisive | ☐ | persistent | ☐ | diplomatic | ☐ |
| aggressive | ☐ | cautious | ☐ | determined | ☐ | responsible | ☐ |
| restless | ☐ | pioneering | ☐ | nonchalant | ☐ | relaxed | ☐ |

**B Adjective formation**

Complete the job reference below with the correct form of the word in brackets.

> As requested, this is an appreciation of Ms Wright who spent four years working in my department. Becker plc is a highly ..................[1] (success) company specialising in precision ..................[2] (science) instruments in a highly ..................[3] (compete) market. During her time with Becker, Ms Wright was ..................[4] (responsibility) for translating ..................[5] (promotion) literature into English. This work requires someone who is ..................[6] (autonomy) and capable of producing ..................[7] (accuracy) translations of both sales information and ..................[8] (technique) documentation. Ms Wright proved to be an extremely ..................[9] (competence) ..................[10] (loyalty) employee and I fully recommend her for the position.

HE'S A DUTIFUL EMPLOYEE, LOYAL AND SUBMISSIVE, BUT HE TENDS TO GET AGGRESSIVE IF YOU TRY TO TAKE AWAY HIS BONE...

MANAGER

## Compound adjectives

### 1 Two-word adjectives

Many adjectives are formed by joining two (or more) words together with a hyphen (-). There are many types of combinations:

adj + noun:   a **small-scale** operation, a **long-term** policy

adj + noun + -*ed*:   a **narrow-minded** approach, a **short-sighted** policy

adj or adv + past participle:   **low-paid** workers, a **well-informed** person

adj, adv, noun + present participle:   a **record-breaking** year, a **problem-solving** approach, a **high-flying** professional, a **far-reaching** effect

noun + adj:   a **tax-free** salary, a **brand-new** product

A few compound adjectives consist of three words:

the **day-to-day** organisation     **up-to-date** information

an **out-of-court** settlement     a **down-to-earth** approach

### 2 Prefixes and suffixes

Some prefixes and suffixes have productive uses; they can combine with many other words to form new words. Here are just a few:

**anti-:** anti-democratic   anti-nuclear   anti-social

**extra-:** extra-large   extra-soft   extra-special

**self-:** self-defeating   self-imposed   self-regulating

**well-:** well-attended   well-known   well-respected

**-based:** London-based   city-based   overseas-based

**-minded:** open-minded   like-minded   single-minded

**-oriented:** market-oriented   consumer-oriented   export-oriented

**-rich:** asset-rich   cash-rich   oil-rich

### 3 Adjectives + nouns

Some adjectives are frequently found with certain nouns and form a relatively fixed word partnership:

We have a **joint account** at the bank.

After a **heated discussion** he stormed out of the meeting.

We're facing **keen competition** from cheap imports.

The outcome was a **foregone conclusion**; everyone knew what would happen.

The biggest **stumbling block** to a peace settlement is the disputed frontier.

Profit-sharing gives everybody a **vested interest** in the company's success.

They say they would use force only as a **last resort**.

**Practice**

## A  Compound adjectives

Use one word to complete each of these sets of expressions.

**1**

trouble-.................. maintenance
lead-.................... petrol
interest-.................. credit

**4**

..................-thought-out strategy
..................-earned rest
..................-timed intervention

**2**

..................-service restaurant
..................-drive car
..................-made man

**5**

short-.................. contract
medium-.................. investment
long-.................. view

**3**

down-....................goods
free-....................economy
up-..................fashion retailer

**6**

..................-dumping agreement
..................-clockwise movement
..................-social hours

## B  Adjectives and nouns

Join the words on the left with those on the right to form word partnerships. Then complete the sentences below.

| | |
|---|---|
| foregone | interest |
| joint | priority |
| last | exchange |
| heated | account |
| stumbling | conclusion |
| high | competition |
| stiff | resort |
| vested | block |

**1** We won the contract in the face of .................. .

**2** My wife and I have a .................. at the National Bank.

**3** After a .................. of views we agreed to disagree.

**4** Dealing with the Y2K bug was a .................. for most IT managers in 1999.

**5** As a .................. we could sell some assets, but only if all else fails.

**6** The territorial dispute is the main .................. to a peace agreement.

**7** There was no point in having a discussion because the outcome was a .................. .

**8** The tobacco industry has a .................. in claiming that smoking does not damage health.

## Adjective position

Adjectives can be used in two positions: before nouns and after verbs such as: *be, become, seem, appear*:

| | |
|---|---|
| a **high** price | The price seemed **high**. |
| a **famous** writer | The writer became **famous**. |
| an **impossible** situation | The situation appeared **impossible**. |
| an **obvious** solution | The solution was **obvious**. |

Most adjectives can be used both ways. However, some can be used in one way only.

### 1 Adjectives only used before the noun

The **former** chairman was forced to resign.
We only give extended credit as a **last** resort.
The **main** thing is not to worry.
A **joint** venture with an overseas firm can be a **major** advantage.
The **previous** agreement was signed in December 1999.

### 2 Adjectives used after the noun

In the following examples it would be incorrect to put the adjective before the noun:

The funds **allocated** to the project did not cover the expenditure.
The people **questioned** during the survey thought the packaging was good.
The issues **discussed** during the meeting were all resolved.
I'd like to refer to one of the points **raised** during the last meeting.
The goods **ordered** last month have not yet been delivered.
The warning **issued** by the authorities was ignored.

In each of the above examples, *who was / were* or *which was / were* could be inserted:

The funds (which were) **allocated** to the project did not cover the expenditure.
The people (who were) **questioned** during the survey thought the packaging was good.

### 3 Adjectives used in both positions but with a change of meaning

the **present** members of the committee (= those who are members now)
the members of the committee **present** (= those in attendance)

She holds an extremely **responsible** post. (= needing ability and sound judgement)
He is **responsible** for sales in South East Asia. (= is in charge of)

She gave us a long, **involved** explanation. (= complicated)
There is a lot of documentation **involved** in getting a government loan. (= connected)

He is an **outstanding** candidate for the post. (= exceptional)
There are a number of invoices **outstanding**. (= unpaid)

## Practice

**A Which adjective?**

Complete the sentences with these adjectives.

> last   major   former   obvious   present   previous

**1** Mrs Thatcher is a .................... British prime minister.

**2** This is the ................... time I make excuses for him.

**3** The ................... decision was overturned by the committee.

**4** In the ................... situation it's better to act without delay.

**5** The high value of the pound was a ................... problem for British exporters.

**6** The company representative will be ...................; she'll be wearing a red uniform.

**B Before or after the noun?**

Which of the phrases in *italics* is correct?

**1** The *discussed issues /issues discussed* have not been solved.

**2** The *money allocated /allocated money* to the project did not cover costs.

**3** I'd like to go back to one of the *raised points /points raised* by Mr Collins.

**4** The *uniform issued /issued uniform* has not been returned.

**5** The *ordered goods /goods ordered* have finally arrived.

**6** The *women questioned /questioned women* during the survey thought the perfume smelt good.

**7** She is an exceptional woman of *outstanding ability /ability outstanding*.

**8** I don't want to enter into a long, *involved argument /argument involved* about who is to blame.

**C Sentence rearrangement**

The words in the following sentences are in the wrong order. Rewrite them in the correct order.

**1** the the statement by government issued misinterpreted was

**2** the the problems during meeting solved have raised been

**3** you shouldn't the worry main is thing that

**4** me her an impossible to cooperate has refusal in situation put

## Adjectives and adverbs

**1** Adjectives usually describe nouns and adverbs modify verbs (see page 72):

| *Adjectives* | *Adverbs* |
|---|---|
| She's a **good** driver. | She drives **well**. |
| We need an **immediate** answer. | We need an answer **immediately**. |
| She has a **soft** voice. | She speaks **softly**. |

**2** Some adjectives and adverbs have the same form:

| | |
|---|---|
| He's a **fast** talker. | He talks **fast**. (NOT *fastly) |
| Mrs Dyke is a **hard** worker. | She works **hard**. (NOT *hardly) |
| There are **daily** flights. | Flights leave **daily**. |
| We need to make an **early** start. | We need to start **early**. |

**3** Some adjectives end in -*ly* but have no corresponding adverbs:

An electron microscope is a **costly** piece of equipment.
She's a very **friendly** person to work with.
We had a **lively** discussion about the origins of the universe.
I left the firm because of the **miserly** salary.

**4** We can use adverbs to modify adjectives, past participles or other adverbs:

She speaks **extremely fast**.
Such a mistake is **easily made**.
He was wearing a **really colourful** tie.
Their business has been **hugely successful**.
A peaceful solution to the conflict is **increasingly unlikely**.

**5** Some adjectives have two corresponding adverbs:

| | |
|---|---|
| The train from Toledo was **late**. | We haven't seen each other **lately**. (= recently) |
| | The train arrived **late**. |
| Let me ask you a **direct** question. | His ideas are **directly** opposed to mine. |
| | Can we fly **direct** to Chicago**?** |
| There will be a **short** delay**.** | We hope to see you **shortly**. (= soon) |
| | Sales fell **short** of target. |
| Sorry. **Wrong** number. | I was **wrongly** dressed for a formal dinner. |
| | Why does everything go **wrong**? |

## Practice

**A Common mistakes**

Which of these sentences is correct? Correct those that are wrong.

1 She likes driving fast cars.

2 I work hardly because I am highly paid.

3 She's a very friendly person.

4 Everything I do recently seems to go wrongly.

5 We need to start earlily.

6 Dealing with the Y2K problem was a costly business.

7 Time is running shortly.

**B Adverb position**

Complete the text appropriately with these adjectives.

| increasingly   easily   extremely   unfortunately   hugely   deeply   suitably   awfully |
|---|

**TMP**

If there is one certainty in life, it is that things change. And in the modern world things are changing ...................[1] fast. This is especially true in the workplace where there is no longer the concept of a job for life. People are ...................[2] likely to work for many different companies throughout their careers. It is ...................[3] common – and ...................[4] disturbing – for companies to say 'Why should we train staff for them to leave for better jobs?' This is an ...................[5] outmoded concept because staff will move regardless of whether they receive training or not.

So how can individuals be ...................[6] prepared to meet the challenges of change? This is not a question that can be ...................[7] answered, but we at TMP Consultants believe we have developed some ...................[8] successful recipes that will help you get the best out of your employees while they stay with you.

## Prepositions of place and direction

We use prepositions to say where a person or thing is, or their direction.

**1** *about / around* (approximate position)

She's left her briefcase lying **about** somewhere. (she doesn't know exactly where)

**2** *across* (from one side to the other)

He walked **across** the room and looked out of the window.

**3** *at* (precise location)

He's sitting **at** his desk.
The Prime Minister lives **at** 10 Downing Street.

**4** *at* (direction)

Our campaign is aimed **at** the top end of the market.
What are you looking **at**?

**5** *beyond* (limit in direction)

Warning! No unauthorised personnel **beyond** this point.

**6** *by* (close to)

I can see him over there **by** the news stand.

**7** *from* (source)

The cars are imported **from** Slovenia.

**8** *in* (three-dimensional space)

He works **in** the City of London.
She puts everything **in** her handbag.

**9** *on* (two-dimensional line or surface)

London stands **on** the river Thames.
A painting by Miro hangs **on** the boardroom wall.

**10** *round / around* (after turning)

Go straight ahead and the bank is just **round / around** the corner.

**11** *through* (direction between two points in space)

We drove **through** Baltimore on our way to Washington

**12** *to* (movement, destination)

I have to go **to** Prague next week.
A taxi will take you **to** the airport.

## Practice

### A Which preposition?

Label each picture with its appropriate preposition.

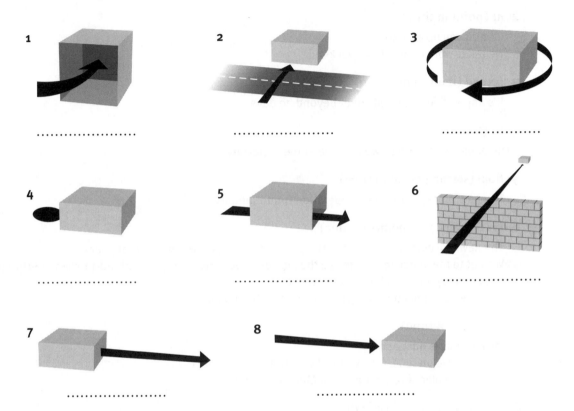

1 ....................

2 ....................

3 ....................

4 ....................

5 ....................

6 ....................

7 ....................

8 ....................

### B Sentence completion

Complete each sentence with a suitable preposition.

1 Why is she always leaving her files lying ...................?

2 Diamonds are imported ................... South Africa.

3 He works ................... the centre of the business district.

4 Cairo stands ................... the River Nile.

5 You can't see it ................... here but the theatre is just ................... the corner.

6 We went ................... Spain on our way ................... France ................... Portugal.

7 She's over there ................... the coffee machine.

8 She lives ................... Amsterdam but is moving ................... The Hague soon.

9 The best restaurant is just ................... the road.

10 From the top of the tower you can see the cathedral and the mountains ................... .

## Prepositions of time

**1** *around / about* (approximately)

She'll get here **around** 11 o'clock.

**2** *at* (point in time)

I'll pick you up **at** 2.30.
He takes work home **at** the weekend.

**3** *beyond* (limit in duration)

It's impossible to extend credit **beyond** 30 days.

**4** *by* (limit in time)

The plane leaves at 9 so we must be at the airport **by** 8am.

**5** *from* (starting point in time)

The new procedure will be in operation **from** 1 January.

**6** *in* (between two points in time)

The new museum was opened to the public **in** 1999. (some time in that year)
We got to the match **in** time to see the kick-off. (we arrived before and didn't miss anything)
They employ temps **in** the summer vacation.
Multimedia applications began to take off **in** the 1990s.

**7** *on* (point of time)

My birthday is **on** 3 April.
Please arrive **on** time. (at exactly the right time, not late)
Our weekly planning meeting is **on** Monday morning.

**8** *through* (direction inside time)

I'll be staying in Florida April **through** June. (American English)
She slept all **through** the meeting.

**9** *to* (future direction)

It's two minutes **to** four.
There are only two weeks **to** the launch.
The store is open from 10 **to** 6.30 every day, except Sunday. (= until)

**10** *until* (limit in time)

We have **until** the end of June to settle the debt.

**Practice**

**A Which preposition?**

Complete the sentences with a suitable preposition of time.

1 Easter falls .................. 5 April this year.

2 He'll be back ................... an hour's time.

3 He took copious notes all ................... the meeting.

4 I'll see you ................... 6 o'clock and make sure you're .................. time!

5 The government privatised massively ................... the 1990s.

6 The financial year runs ................... 1 April ................... 31 March.

7 We arrived just ................... time to see the opening ceremony.

8 This project could take us into 2010 and ................... .

9 You have to send in your tax declaration ................... 15 March at the latest.

10 I don't know what time she'll arrive; ................... 3 o'clock I guess, or a bit later.

**B Prepositions of time**

Look at Mr Cottrell's diary and write sentences to describe the events. Today is 2 May.

Example: *He's coming back from France at 4.45pm on 5 May.*

| | |
|---|---|
| **3 May** | *BA 515 ⟶ Paris, Hotel du Nord* |
| **4 May** | *Meet Monsieur Vatel ( 22 rue Danton)* |
| **5 May** | *Back (16.45 flight)* |
| **6 May** | *Board meeting 10.00 12.30* |
| **7 May** | *Deadline for phone bill* |
| **8 May** | *Jane back from Dublin (11.30 approx)* |
| **9 May** | *Pick Lucy up from her dance lesson (17.00)* |
| **10 May** | *New share option scheme comes into force* |
| **11 May** | *Bill's birthday: dinner party 20.00 24.00* |

# Functions

## Advising

**1** *in my opinion, if I were you, it's worth + verb + -ing, etc.*

**In my opinion**, it would be better to take on temporary staff.
**If I were you**, I'd take the train; it's faster.
**It's worth** try**ing** to get an upgrade.
**My advice** would be to lobby the government.
**In your shoes**, I'd make a strong complaint.
**Why not** do some lateral thinking?

**2** *you'd better*

If you think you won't understand **you'd better** use an interpreter.

*'d* is an abbreviation of *had* and not *would*. Note that the verb following *'d better* is used without *to*:

**You'd better** ask her for her permission before you go ahead. (NOT *to ask her)
**You'd better** not use the software without a site licence. (NOT *to use, *to not use)

**3** Using the imperative

**Be** nice to her.
**Think** about it first.
**Remember** to take your passport.
**Make sure** you take enough money.

If the situation is dangerous the advice is more like a warning:

**Be** careful.
**Check** your tyres before setting off on a long journey.

**4** Using a negative form with *don't*

These statements offer advice in the form of a command:

**Don't get** discouraged.
**Don't be** afraid to take risks.

The examples below function more as a warning:

**Don't do** anything without telling your boss first.
**Don't buy** shares in BKI – they're about to go into liquidation.

 *Giving instructions page 128, for another use of the imperative*

**Practice**

**A Giving advice**

Complete the second sentence so that it means more or less the same as the first.

**1** You'd better hurry or you'll miss the plane.

If you ..................................................................................................................................

**2** In my opinion, it would be better to sell your shares now.

My advice ............................................................................................................................

**3** It's not a good idea to drive through the city centre during rush hour.

Don't ...................................................................................................................................

**4** Why don't you see a doctor if you're feeling ill?

You'd ...................................................................................................................................

**5** I don't think it's advisable to tell her the bad news yet.

You'd ...................................................................................................................................

**6** In my opinion, you ought to declare your overseas investments to the tax authorities.

If I .......................................................................................................................................

**7** It's a good idea to ask for a second opinion.

It's worth ............................................................................................................................

**B If I were you ...**

You work for a firm of consultants that deals with personnel and training issues. What would be your advice in the following situation?

Mr Mudd has been working in the same bank for 20 years and in Customer Relations for the past 15. He has had some temporary postings in other sections and once worked as a replacement in another branch. His job involves applying rules to routine cases and although his performance is competent and reliable, he is unwilling to take the initiative.

His work is basically that of a clerk but because of his length of service he earns quite a lot more than other, younger employees who do much the same kind of work. He recently turned down the opportunity to train to become a branch manager, saying 'I'm happy in my job and I enjoy working in a team. I don't want to be in charge'.

## Agreeing and disagreeing

You can use the following words and expressions depending on the formality of the situation.

**1 Agreeing**

| *More formal* | *Informal* |
|---|---|
| I completely / entirely / totally agree. | Right. |
| Yes, definitely. | Sure. |
| Yes, I'd go along with that. | Fine. |
| Yes, I agree with that wholeheartedly. | Great. |
| (NOT *I am agree with you.) | |

**2 Disagreeing**

| *More formal* | *Informal* |
|---|---|
| I don't agree. | Ridiculous. |
| (NOT *I am not agree.) | No way. |
| I can't go along with that. | Over my dead body! |
| I disagree with that completely. | You're joking. |
| For me that is out of the question. | |

**3** *So do I / Neither do I*, etc.

If you are in agreement with someone or have something in common, you can use *so* or *neither* to replace the noun phrase:

| | |
|---|---|
| **I'm** very interested in archaeology. | So **am** I. |
| I **can't** stand waiting in airports. | Neither **can** I. |
| My wife and I **play** tennis a lot. | So **do** we. |
| **I'll** be going to London soon. | So **will** I. |
| I **don't** believe in politicians. | Neither **do** I. |

**4 Shades of opinion**

You may have mixed feelings or not hold a strong opinion either way. In that case you can express a doubt or reservation:

I agree with you **to some extent** but ...
Yes, I'd go along with that **up to a point** but ...
That **may well be the case** although ...
You **may have a point** but ...
Yes, but **on the other hand** ...
Maybe, but we **still have to remember** that ...

Sometimes, especially in British English, these expressions are used to show politeness when you actually disagree but want to acknowledge the other speaker's contribution.

**Practice**

**A** *so / neither*

Read the statements made by several speakers and agree with them, using *so* or *neither*.

Example:

'I'm tired.' ....*So am I.*......

**1** 'I didn't like *Jurassic Park*.' ....................

**2** 'I can't stand people who are rude.' ....................

**3** 'I should really exercise more.' ....................

**4** 'I've never been to Fiji.' ....................

**5** 'I enjoy going to the theatre.' ....................

**6** 'I generally take a holiday in the summer.' ....................

**B** Shades of opinion

How do you feel about the following? Write your ideas with a suitable expression of agreement or disagreement, as in the example.

|  | I agree entirely. | I agree to some extent. | I don't really agree. | I completely disagree. |
|---|---|---|---|---|
| **1** All men and women should do military service. |  |  |  |  |
| **2** There should be a single world currency. |  |  |  |  |
| **3** National industries should be protected. |  | *Yes, I'd go along with that up to a point but you can't ignore market forces entirely.* |  |  |
| **4** Smoking at work should be banned. |  |  |  |  |
| **5** Men and women should retire at 55. |  |  |  |  |

## Asking for information

**1** Asking for a *Yes* or *No* response

All these questions use an *auxiliary* as the first word in the question and require a positive (*Yes*) or negative (*No*) answer:

| | |
|---|---|
| **Is** Mohammed in his office? | Yes, he is. |
| **Can** you speak Arabic? | No, I can't. |
| **Are** you ready? | No, I'm not. |
| **Do** you belong to a union? | No, I don't. |
| **Does** your firm have a language policy? | No, it doesn't. |
| **Has** she finished the report? | Yes, she has. |
| **Have** the goods arrived at the frontier? | No, they haven't yet. |
| **Should** we have complained? | Yes, definitely. |
| **Did** they give a discount? | No, they didn't actually. |
| **Will** they change the price? | No, they won't. |

**2** Open questions

We use this question form when we want more information than a simple confirmation or denial:

| | |
|---|---|
| **When** will the order be sent? | **Which** is the best area to live in? |
| **Where** would you like to work? | **Why** is he never on time? |
| **Who** is in charge of human resources? | **Whose** car is blocking the entrance? |
| **What** brand of washing powder do you use? | **How** have you changed in the last five years? |

The question word is placed before the auxiliary verb.

When we use a verb in a simple tense (present or past) we have to use the auxiliary *do / does / did* or a modal (*can / will / should*, etc.):

| | |
|---|---|
| **Where do** you live? | **Who should** I ask for? |
| **Where can** I get a taxi? | **Why didn't** they come? |
| **When does** she want it? | **Why couldn't** she do it? |
| **When shall** I arrive? | **Where did** you get it from? |
| **Who do** you work with? | **Where would** you like to go? |

**3** Negative questions

We use a negative question when we suspect the answer will be *No,* having first thought it would be *Yes.*

**Can't** you get there earlier? (I think it's possible)
**Didn't** you tell them about the deal? (I thought you would)
**Won't** 8 o'clock be too late? (I suspect it will be)
**Aren't** you going to the conference? (I thought you were)

**4** *Who, what* and *which*

When *who, what* or *which* is the *subject* of a sentence, an auxiliary is not used:

**Who wants** a lift to the station? (NOT *Who does want ...)
**What happened** at the meeting? (NOT *What did happen ...)
**Which costs** more? (NOT *Which does cost more?)

## Practice

**A Asking questions**

Fill in this questionnaire by writing the correct question forms.

| Subject | Question | Answer |
|---|---|---|
| **1** NAME | .........*what*... is your name? | Per Lysvag. |
| **2** STATUS | .................... you single or married? | I'm separated. |
| **3** ADDRESS | .................... do you live? | In Coventry. |
| **4** AGE | .................... are you? | 27. |
| **5** OCCUPATION | .................... do you do for a living? | I'm an engineer. |
| **6** LENGTH OF SERVICE | .................... have you been working for your present employer? | Three years. |
| **7** SALARY | .................... do you earn? | £40, 000 a year. |
| **8** FOREIGN TRAVEL | .................... do you go abroad? | Three or four times a year, mostly back to Sweden. |
| **9** ENGLISH AT WORK | .................... did you last have to make a presentation in English? | Last week at a meeting in Birmingham. |
| **10** REASON FOR LANGUAGE TRAINING | .................... do you need training in foreign languages? | To speak with my colleagues and customers abroad. |
| **11** LANGUAGE ABILITY | .................... of these words describes your ability in English: beginner, intermediate or advanced? | Advanced, I hope! |

**B A bad line**

Sue Watson is phoning Bill Daniels about a recent open day but her mobile phone battery is low and sometimes she can't be heard. Write the questions Bill has to ask.

**Sue** It was a great success. More than **xxxxx** people visited the plant.

**Bill** Sorry. ....................................[1] the plant?

**Sue** Over 2,000. And **xxxxx** congratulated you on your excellent organisation!

**Bill** I can't hear you. ....................................[2] me?

**Sue** The **xxxxx** Director complimented you on your organisation.

**Bill** Sorry? ....................................[3] complimented me?

**Sue** The Divisional Director. Look, it's a really bad line. I'll talk to you later.

## Comparing products and services

There are many ways of making a comparison between one thing and another. For example:

The cost of living is **higher** in Tokyo **than** in Bucharest.
Tokyo is **the most expensive** city in the world.
In 2000 one euro was worth **about as much as** one US dollar.

This article contains a large number of comparative and superlative expressions. They are all in bold type:

From cars to cans of beer, UK consumers pay **more than** their counterparts elsewhere in Europe. Now, for the first time in 20 years, the British government is showing **more than** a passing interest in the prices British citizens pay.

The strength of the pound may explain why a CD or a mobile phone bought in France is **cheaper than** in the UK. But the currency factor does not explain why a Sony Trinitron TV costs **£77 more** in London **than** in Paris. Nor does it explain why a bottle of Chanel No. 5 costs **a third more** in Britain **than** in France, when the strong pound should make imported goods **less expensive than** they would otherwise be.

But there are some good reasons for price differences. For example, none of the American branded goods manufacturers make **more profit** in the UK **than** in the US. Shelf-price comparisons are misleading. New York prices are quoted before federal and state taxes **whereas** VAT is included in the UK. Distribution and marketing costs are **much higher** in Europe **than** in the US.

Product literature must be produced in many languages with the result that producing the manuals for TV sets in Europe costs **as much as** the glass in the television screen.

Rents are an issue too. British rents are high **compared with** other countries. In the US, rents are **lower** because there are **fewer** planning controls. It is simply a **bigger** country and, on average, selling space in the UK costs **40 per cent more than** in the US. Labour costs are **lower** too.

British supermarkets are often attacked for their profit margins which average 6 per cent, **the highest** in Europe and **three times more than** the levels achieved by their European rivals. But there is **no worse** example **than** the car industry. A recent survey identified the UK as **the most expensive** place in Europe to buy a car. British drivers are asked to pay up to **52 per cent more than** on the continent for exactly **the same** car and average UK prices are **16 per cent more than** comparable cars in the Eurozone.

From *The Guardian*

## Practice

### A Making comparisons

Match the ways in which comparisons can be made with the examples on the right.

1  comparative adjective + *than*
2  *more / less* + adjective + *than*
3  *more* + noun + *than*
4  *as* + quantifier + *as*
5  *a* + comparative adjective + noun
6  numeral + *more than*
7  quantifier + comparative adjective + *than*
8  a superlative

a) as much as
b) cheaper than in the UK
c) the highest / the most expensive
d) less expensive than
e) much higher than
f) more profit than
g) a bigger country
h) £77 more than

### B Common mistakes

Correct the errors in these sentences.

1  Lisbon is not as big than London.
2  There is more to life that a spreadsheet.
3  The advantage of this project is that it is twice cheaper than the other.
4  Women's pay used to be more lower than men's, even for a same work.
5  Metro is the world's second bigger retailer after Wal-Mart Stores of the US.

### C The top headhunting firms

Look at the table and complete the following paragraph with these expressions.

a little less   the largest   much more   most strongly   even closer

| Net revenue ($m) | | | |
| --- | --- | --- | --- |
| | 1997 | 1998 | % change |
| Korn Ferry International | 315 | 350 | +11 |
| Heidrick & Struggles | 263 | 324 | +23 |
| Spencer Stuart | 219 | 240 | +10 |
| Egon Zehnder | 182 | 218 | +20 |
| Russell Reynolds | 184 | 196 | +7 |

Among the top five headhunting firms worldwide, Korn Ferry International, the industry leader, is still ..................[1] firm in terms of net revenue. However, Heidrick & Struggles grew ..................[2] in 1998, edging ..................[3] to Korn Ferry. In fourth position, Egon Zehnder increased its revenues by 20%, just ..................[4] than Heidrick & Struggles but ..................[5] than Russell Reynolds, which posted a change of just 7%.

From the *Financial Times*

## Complaining and apologising

**1 Complaining to someone you know well**

If you are annoyed at someone's behaviour you can say:

**I'm fed up with** your attitude.
**I've had enough of** it.
**I wish you wouldn't** ...
**I'd rather you didn't** ...

If your complaint mentions the person concerned we use a pronoun + verb + *-ing*:

**I'm fed up with him** tell**ing** me what to do all the time.
**I'm sick (to death) of them** complain**ing**.

You can also use *always* + the present progressive to express your annoyance:

You**'re always** try**ing** to control what I do.
You**'re** always mak**ing** such a fuss.

**2 Taking a complaint further**

If you have already complained and nothing has been done then you can say:

**I want to see** the manager / person in charge.
**I'm afraid I'm not satisfied with** the standard of service.
**I'd like to make a (formal) complaint** about the hygiene.

**3 Complaining in writing**

You can start your letter in a number of ways:

I regret to have to complain about ...
I am writing to complain about ...
I am writing to express my concern about ...
I would like to make a complaint about ...

**4 Threatening**

In order to back up your complaint you can promise to do something unpleasant if you do not receive satisfaction. You can make a threat by using *if* or *unless*:

**Unless** I receive compensation I will have to take legal action.
I would be reluctant to change suppliers, but **if** the situation does not improve I will be forced to look elsewhere.

 *Conditionals* page 34

**5 Apologising**

In speech it is common to say *I'm sorry / I'm extremely sorry for* (*the delay*).

In writing, you can put:

We (sincerely) apologise for the misunderstanding.
I assure you we are doing everything in our power to put things right.
I fully appreciate your position and very much regret the inconvenience this has caused.

**Practice**

## A A letter of complaint

The sentences in this letter of complaint have been jumbled. Put them back into the correct order and insert these words and expressions.

| I am writing to express my concern    Regrettably,    I will have no alternative but to |
|---|

Dear Mrs O'Malley,

However, if the delay continues ...................[1] give instructions to suspend payment of your last invoice.

...................[2] about the failure to supply the essential components which were promised us for 1 April and which do not seem to have reached us.

Given the long-standing relationship between our two firms I would be reluctant to change suppliers.

I look forward to your response.

...................[3] this delay is now causing a botttleneck in our production.

Yours sincerely,

## B A letter of apology

This is the fax that was sent by Mrs O'Malley in reply. Complete it with these phrases.

| We very much regret    Once again, we apologise    We are very concerned<br>hope you will understand the reason    I assure you we are doing everything in our power |
|---|

...................[1] to hear that the consignment of spare parts that was ordered from us in February has not reached you. ...................[2] the disruption this has caused to your production.

...................[3] to make sure the consignment arrives as soon as possible. The delay is due to an expected delivery of components from Spain which has been held up as a result of industrial unrest. However, the components have now arrived and the consignment has been sent to you airfreight.

...................[4] for the inconvenience and ...................[5].

From the *Financial Times*

# Confirming information

Question tags are used when we expect the person we are speaking to to agree with us or confirm that what we are saying is right. They are most often used in spoken English.

**Form**  Tags are formed using an auxiliary and the pronoun referring to the subject. The tag is almost always contracted.

| Affirmative main clause | Negative tag |
|---|---|
| It**'s** hot today, | **isn't** it? |
| You **were** there, | **weren't** you? |
| You**'re** Canadian, | **aren't** you? |
| She **can** drive, | **can't** she? |
| You **will** stay in touch, | **won't** you? |

| Negative main clause | Positive tag |
|---|---|
| The meeting **isn't** today, | **is** it? |
| She **wasn't** present, | **was** she? |
| They**'re not** coming, | **are** they? |
| She **shouldn't** know, | **should** she? |
| She **couldn't** get there, | **could** she? |

If the main clause does not have an auxiliary or the verb *to be*, we use *do*, *does* or *did* in the tag:

You **agree** with me, **don't** you?     She **gave** you her number, **didn't** she?
You **don't like** raw fish, **do** you?     He **doesn't drink** alcohol, **does** he?

When *have* is used for states (e.g. possession) both *do* and *have* are used for the tag in British English but *do* is normal in American English.

You have a motorbike, don't you / haven't you?
Your father has a yacht, doesn't he / hasn't he?

The tag for *I am* is *aren't I?*

I**'m** not late, **am** I?     I**'m** late, **aren't** I?

**Uses**  **1 Asking a real question**

If we really want an answer to the question, the voice goes up at the end of the question:
The meeting's at 10 o'clock, isn't it?     You do agree, don't you?

**2 Asking for agreement**

If the question is not a real one, we use falling intonation:
It's a nice day, isn't it?     You have to wait a long time, don't you?

**3 Making offers or suggestions**

I**'ll** get you a drink, **shall I**?     **Let's** pencil in Thursday, **shall we**?

**4 Agreement**

'It's hot today, isn't it?' 'Yes, it is.'
'The meeting isn't today, is it?' 'No, it isn't.'

**Practice**

### A Confirming decisions

The people taking part in the conversation below are trying to remember what was said during a recent meeting. Complete the dialogue using appropriate question tags.

**A** What did we say Janice was going to do?

**B** Janice was going to revise the estimates, ...................[1]?

**C** I think so. And she said she would talk to Aziz about it, ...................[2]?

**A** Are you sure?

**B** Perhaps. But Bill wanted to change the procedure, ...................[3]?

**C** He didn't say that, ...................[4]?

**B** I thought he did. But it wouldn't work, ...................[5]? We agreed on that, ...................[6]?

**A** I can't remember, to be honest. We should have taken notes, ...................[7]?

**B** Yes, it's terrible, ...................[8]? We'd better have the meeting again, ...................[9]?

**A** OK, let's make it first thing Monday morning, ...................[10]?

**C** OK by me.

### B A conversation at a cocktail party

Complete the following conversation which takes place at a cocktail reception held at an embassy.

**A** Hello, you're Mick Harvey, ...................[1]?

**B** That's right. How do you know my name?

**A** You were the commercial attaché in Egypt.

**B** That's right. Oh yes, and you were working for Amoco, ...................[2]?

**A** Yes, but I left six months ago.

**B** The weather's wonderful, ...................[3]?

**A** Too hot for me. Is that the ambassador over there?

**B** Yes. You've met him, ...................[4]?

**A** No, actually I haven't.

**B** Well, I'll introduce you, ...................[5]?

## Describing a company

Read this extract from Nestlé Management Report 1999 and note how the information is organised:

Nestlé, whose head office is in Vevey on the shores of Lake Geneva, is the world's largest food company. Although it is Switzerland's biggest industrial enterprise, only 2% of sales are generated in Switzerland. We are a truly global company employing 230,929 people on every continent. Consequently, our management and staff reflect a truly international outlook.

Nestlé now produces the world's favourite brands in 509 factories worldwide. In over 130 years of growth and diversification, we have never lost sight of our core business: improving the quality of people's lives through high-quality, nutritious, and convenient prepared foods and beverages. Today, Nestlé brands are present on almost every supermarket shelf, and some products – like NESCAFE, NESTLE, NESTEA, BUITONI, MAGGI AND FRISKIES – are sold in more than 100 countries.

| | |
|---|---|
| *Geography*: | multinational, head office in Switzerland |
| *Employees*: | 230,929 people on five continents |
| *Activity*: | the world's largest food company, producing global brands |
| *Production facilities*: | 509 factories worldwide |
| *Financial information*: | market capitalisation 112,032 million Swiss francs |

Other useful phrases include:

| | |
|---|---|
| *Geography*: | We are based in / located in / situated in ... |
| *Employees*: | We employ (n) people / there are (n) people on the payroll |
| *Activity*: | Our firm specialises in / produces / manufactures / supplies ... |
| *Type*: | a joint venture |
| | a subsidiary |
| | a holding company |
| *Position*: | is the leading company in its field |
| | ranks number one in the market for ... |
| | is a major player / operates in many different markets |
| | is a group ranking among the world's top 20 .... |
| | recently established |
| | well-established |
| | with a long tradition of success |
| *Financial information*: | achieving annual turnover of $(n) |
| | accounts for (n)% of sales |
| | generates profits of (n) |

**A HMV**

Complete the following extract using these words.

| operates | worldwide | the world's foremost | comprises | leading |

HMV Media Group plc .................¹ HMV, one of .................² specialist music retailers, and Waterstones and Dillons, the two .................³ brands in the UK book retailing market. The group .................⁴ in many different markets with over 470 stores .................⁵, generating sales of over £1 billion.

**B Wieden & Kennedy**

Complete the following extract using these words.

| headquarters | range | world-class | employs | headquartered | located | operations |

Wieden & Kennedy is a .................¹ advertising agency, .................² in the USA with .................³ all over the globe. Its clients .................⁴ from Coca-Cola to Microsoft and Nike. Wieden & Kennedy's European .................⁵ is .................⁶ in Amsterdam and .................⁷ approximately 120 people.

**C Sita**

Using the information in the box write a description of Sita as the first paragraph for the job advertisement below.

| | |
|---|---|
| *Geography*: | Geneva-based; present in 225 countries (900+ locations) |
| *Staff*: | 5,000+ |
| *Activity*: | telecommunications (70,000 customer connections) |
| *Position*: | largest communications network |
| *Revenues*: | £1 billion |

# INTERNATIONAL TAX MANAGER

.............................................................................

.............................................................................

.............................................................................

- SITA provides a one-stop shop for all mission-critical business-to-business communications and information needs.

- Our client is seeking to recruit a tax specialist who has a strong track record in practice and/or commerce/industry.

From the *Financial Times*

## Describing processes

### Focusing on information

When describing a process, we focus more on what is done than on who does it. For this reason, the passive is commonly used, as in the passage below on recycling.

Recyclable materials **are recovered** from municipal refuse by a number of methods, including shredding (cutting and tearing things into long, thin strips), separating metals with a large magnet, screening and washing. Another method of recovery is the wet pulping process. Incoming refuse **is mixed** with water and **ground** into a pulp in a machine called the wet pulper, which resembles a large kitchen disposal unit. Large pieces of metal are pulled out by a magnetic device before everything from the pulper **is loaded** into a centrifuge called a liquid cyclone. Here the heavier materials which cannot be burnt, such as glass, metals and ceramics, **are separated** out and **sent** on to a glass- and metal-recovery system. Other, lighter materials go to a paper-fibre-recovery system. The final residue **is** either **burnt** or **is used** as landfill.

### Mixing active and passive verb forms

It is also possible to mention what actions people or things perform in a process as well as focusing on the action itself. So there is a mixture of active and passive.

Creating a news story

Whenever a disaster happens somewhere in the world, reporters and photographers are sent there to interview people and take pictures. The news reports are sent by e-mail or over the phone and the rolls of film rushed back to the office to be developed.

Then other journalists type up the stories and the pictures are scanned into the computer. Designers work on the stories and photos on-screen in order to get the layout right. The computer prints out the page of news onto a piece of clear film which is laid on a light-sensitive plate and exposed to a brief flash of light.

A plate is made for each page of the newspaper, wrapped around a roller on the printing press and coated with ink. When all the pages have been printed they are put together in the right order. The finished newspapers are finally tied into bundles and delivered to news-stands.

 *Passives (2) page 50*

## Practice

**A Active or passive?**

Complete this passage using either active or passive forms of the verb.

Manufacturing resource planning – MRP – is a process which ..................[1] (integrate) marketing, production and sales. MRP ..................[2] (rely) upon a fully integrated process and ..................[3] (coordinate) by a master scheduler, who ..................[4] (ensure) that each of the three phases ..................[5] (manage) cost-effectively and efficiently.

In MRP, all the projections, estimates and forecasts have to ..................[6] (synthesise) in a production plan into concrete stages and mixes of products, whose manufacture has to ..................[7] (schedule) as cost-effectively as possible, using just-in-time and electronic data interchange systems. Each stage in the production process ..................[8] (give) a separate coding. Thus all arriving raw materials or bought-in parts ..................[9] (check) for quality and will not ..................[10] (use) until set standards have ..................[11] (meet). Similarly, finished goods may not ..................[12] (warehouse) until quality checks have ..................[13] (fulfil). At each stage all materials and items ..................[14] (give) unique production batch codings for identification in case of a defect occurring. In this way a computer database ..................[15] (build up) of each and every production run. In the case of a product recall, any defect problems may ..................[16] (locate) quickly and the public relations damage will therefore ..................[17] (limit).

*From Business: A Student's Guide*

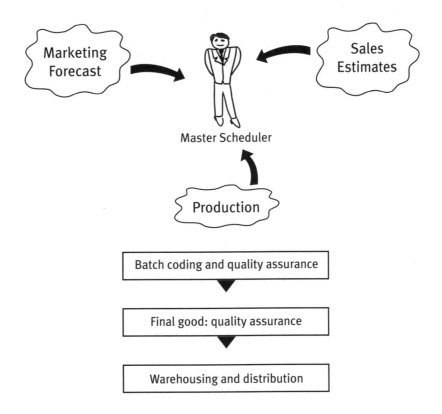

Marketing Forecast

Sales Estimates

Master Scheduler

Production

Batch coding and quality assurance

Final good: quality assurance

Warehousing and distribution

## Describing trends

### 1 Present trends

When we describe a trend, we describe a changing, developing situation. Therefore, to describe ongoing trends we use either the present progressive (  page 10) or the present perfect progressive ( page 26).

People **are living** longer.
The number of single-parent families **is increasing**.
People **are eating** more and more convenience foods and drinking more wine than ever before.
The proportion of a family's income spent on entertainment **has been rising**.

### 2 Trends that began in the past and have reached an end-point

We use the present perfect when a trend has come to completion:
The re-engineering of our firm **has created** a flatter hierarchy.
The European consumer **has become** more sophisticated.

### 3 How long?

If you want to say how long a trend has lasted, you can use a number of time expressions.

We use *during* or *in*, *from* and *until* with periods in the past:
**During** the late 1990s companies were getting ready for the Y2K bug.
The world slumped into depression **in** the 1930s.
**From** the mid-1980s government spending tended to go down.
Things were going well **until** the Asian stock market crash.

Time up to the present can be expressed using *for*, *since* and *over*:
We've been targeting a different market segment **for** the last two years. (*for* + duration)
They've been heading for a fall **since** last February. (*since* + point in time)
We've increased our market share **over** the last five years. (from five years ago up to now)

**Practice**

## A Trends in consumer relationships

Read the extract and decide whether the trends described have reached an end-point or are still developing. Then choose a suitable form for the verbs in brackets. There may be more than one possible answer.

In the days before mass marketing, the local bank manager knew the names and ages of his customers' children, the corner shop knew which brand of breakfast cereal to stock for local families and businessmen bought their suits tailor-made.

But all that ................. [1] (change). Today, under the onslaught of cost-cutting, rationalisation and automation, many people ................. [2] (never see) their bank manager, an impersonal supermarket checkout ................. [3] (replace) the cosy corner shop and most people ................. [4] (never have) a suit made to measure.

Further radical change is under way. More and more companies ................. [5] (realise) that the conventional mass-production model on which consumer marketing ................. [6] (base) no longer works.

Instead of focusing narrowly on cost-cutting measures and improving efficiency, more and more market leaders ................. [7] (re-examine) their business strategies and deciding that customer services and customer relationship management are the keys to future growth.

Increasingly, companies ................. [8] (take) a holistic view of their customer relationships and focusing on the lifetime value of those relationships. It costs five to eight times more to acquire a customer than it does to retain an existing one. Consequently customer relationship management – CRM for short – ................. [9] (become) one of the hottest new fields of consultancy.

From the *Financial Times*

## B Describing trends

Write sentences describing the trends in the graphs below. Use one or more of the time expressions on the previous page.

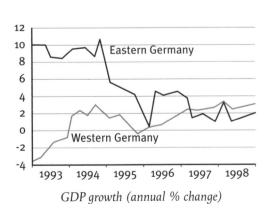

*GDP growth (annual % change)*

From the *Financial Times*

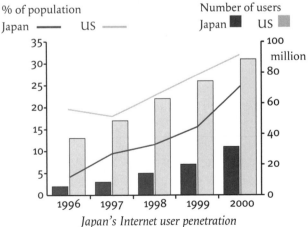

*Japan's Internet user penetration*

From the *Financial Times*

## Forecasting and speculating

### 1 Forecasting

We use *will* to make predictions about the future:

In the future everybody **will** be famous for 15 minutes. (Andy Warhol)
A manned spacecraft **will** land on Mars in the next 20 years or so.

⬤ *Future* page 28

We use *likely to* if we think something is probably going to happen and *bound to* if we are 100% certain:

My memory's getting worse so I'm **likely to** forget.
He hasn't done any work at all. He's **bound to** fail his examination.

### 2 Speculating

We use *if* + past simple + conditional to make a hypothesis about the future:

If I **knew** how the stock markets were going to react, I **would** get rich.
If work **was** such a splendid thing, the rich **would** keep more of it for themselves.

⬤ *Conditionals* page 34

We use modal verbs to make deductions about present situations:

He left an hour ago and it's not far so he **will** / **must** be there by now. (100% certain)
He left 45 minutes ago and it's not far so he **should** be there by now. (reasonably certain)
He left 30 minutes ago and it's not far so he **may** / **might** be there by now. (possible but uncertain)
He only left 15 minutes ago and it's quite far so he **can't** / **won't** be there yet. (impossible)

⬤ *Modal verbs* page 52

### 3 Speculating about the past

We use *if* + past perfect + conditional to make a hypothesis about the past:

If he **had got** better grades at school he **would have gone** to university.
If I **hadn't been** in the right place at the right time I **wouldn't have got** the opportunity.

*Must* and *can't* are also used to make suppositions about the past:

The door was locked so the thieves **must have got in** through the window.
I wasn't there myself but the atmosphere **must have been** electric.
He says he met me in Brussels but he **can't have** – I've never been there.
She looked so surprised when I arrived, she **can't have been expecting** me.

**A Forecasting**

What is in store for you, your company and your country? Write sentences using *bound to*, *likely to* or *unlikely to* about the following.

1 a pay rise

2 a takeover

3 redundancy

4 promotion

5 a change of government in the next six months

**B Speculating**

Match the sentence halves and complete the blanks with *must* or *can't*.

1 She looks so young;

2 She can speak English and Spanish perfectly;

3 She ................... know what's in the report;

4 She ................... have friends in high places

5 She ................... know Berlin pretty well;

6 She ................... have much of a social life;

a) she ................. come from a bilingual family.

b) she ....*can't*........ be a day over 30.

c) she works 60 hours a week.

d) she lived there for three years.

e) she hasn't had a copy.

f) because she's survived three major scandals.

**C Making hypotheses**

What can you infer about these situations?

1 The director suddenly bought a huge block of shares when everybody else was selling theirs. Then the share price soared by 25%.

2 The fish in the canteen smelt strange yesterday and subsequently a number of employees have not reported for work.

3 She insists that he spoke to her in Urdu but he's never learnt a word of Urdu in his life.

4 There is an unexplained loss of £1.5 million in the company accounts and the finance director has been absent from work for the last eight days.

## Getting things done

**1** If we arrange for something to be done by someone else, we say that we *get* or *have* them done for us. *Have* is slightly more formal:

| Subject | get /have | Object | Past participle |
|---|---|---|---|
| We | **are getting** | our offices | **redecorated**. |
| Could you | **have** | this payment | **authorised** by the accounts department? |
| They | **get** | their catalogue | **printed** in Mexico. |
| We've always | **had** | the machines | **assembled** on another site. |

**2** We can use *have* followed by an object + base form of the verb if we want to emphasise who does or did the work we arranged:

I always **have** my secretary **check** my spelling.
I **had** the maintenance people **test** the air conditioning.
She **had** the catering staff **prepare** a meal for the guests.

If we want to use *get* we use an object + *to*-infinitive:

I always **get** my secretary **to check** my spelling.
I **got** the maintenance people **to test** the air conditioning.
She **got** the catering staff **to prepare** a meal for the guests.

**3** There are a number of verbs that describe action undertaken to make sure something is done:

attend to    contend with    cope with    deal with    follow up (on)
handle    process    see to    tackle    take care of

Mrs Baker **deals with** all requests for product information.
It's my job to **see to** all routine maintenance work.
There are a lot of things to **attend to** before the trade fair.
You should allow three working days for your order to be **processed**.
It is our policy to **follow up on** all customer complaints.
Her assistant is ill and I don't know how she is **coping with** the extra workload.

## Practice

**A Getting things done**

Rewrite the sentences using *have* or *get*. Decide whether or not you want to emphasise who does or did the work.

1 All our export risks are insured.

We ...............................................................................................................

2 The garage services my car every 15,000 kilometres.

I ...............................................................................................................

3 A specialist agency translates all the company documentation and manuals. (two possible answers)

We ...............................................................................................................

We...............................................................................................................

4 We've asked the contractors to build a new extension. (two possible answers)

We're ...............................................................................................................

We're ...............................................................................................................

5 The legal department drew up the contract on my instructions. (two possible answers)

I ...............................................................................................................

I ...............................................................................................................

**B Arranging for things to be done**

React to the statements below using the word in brackets, as in the example.

Example:

My passport expires soon. (renew)
*I need to have it renewed.* ...............................................................................................................

1 The printer only works sporadically. (fix)

...............................................................................................................

2 Mrs Baxter is going on a training course. (replace)

...............................................................................................................

3 The outside windows are incredibly dirty. (clean)

...............................................................................................................

4 I'm not sure the figures are entirely accurate. (check)

...............................................................................................................

## Giving instructions

1  **Using the imperative**

We use the base form of the verb to give instructions and issue warnings, as in the following extract from a technical manual.

- **Turn** the pump pressure off at the control panel.
- **Hold** the gun over an appropriate empty container and **lock** the gun in an open position.
- **Remove** the injector.
- **Disconnect** the air supply from the system.

 **DANGER:**

**Do not attempt** to remove, repair or clean an accumulator until you have relieved pressure.

- Using your hand, **unscrew** the filter tank from the filter body (see figure 66).

  ⚠ **Do not use** a wrench.

- **Remove** the filter core and the screen from the filter tank (see figure 67).
- **Inspect** the filter core and screen, then **clean** with solvent.

2  **Using the present simple**

The following instructions mix the imperative and the present simple:

This is how you get to our office from the train station. Turn left as you come out and walk down Richmond Street. You continue for about 100 metres and turn right at the bank. You then cross over the canal and you will see a high-rise office building in front of you. We are on the seventh floor.

3  **Giving special instructions**

You can stress the importance of your instructions by prefacing them with a number of phrases:

**Make sure you** wear appropriate protective clothing.
**Do not forget to** turn off the electricity supply before opening the panel.
**Always** use the correct lubricating fluid.
**Never** clean your clothing with compressed air.

## Practice

**A** Changing a wheel

Match the pictures to the instructions and put them in the correct order.

- [ ] Lower the vehicle and remove the jack.
- [ ] Tighten the wheel bolts.
- [ ] Replace the centre hub cap.
- [ ] Unscrew the wheel bolts.
- [ ] Prise out the centre hub cap.
- [1] Park ther car on a flat, stable surface and apply the handbrake firmly. *C*
- [ ] Remove the wheel and replace it with the spare.
- [ ] Raise the vehicle off the ground with a jack.

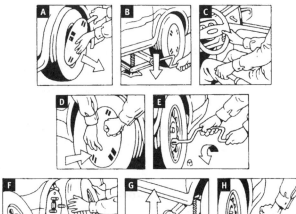

**B** Giving directions

Debbie Scott works as a secretary. Her new divisional manager has to go to the London headquarters next week to attend a meeting and he has decided to drive there.

Debbie is ringing another secretary, Judith, to get exact directions. Trace the route on the map and mark where the headquarters are located.

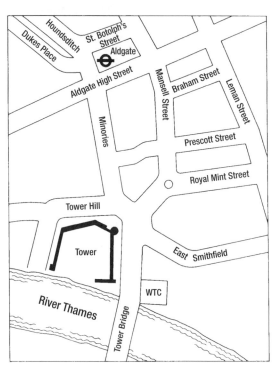

**Judith** I think his best bet is to follow the signs to Central London and the City and cross the Thames at Tower Bridge.

**Debbie** ... signs to Central London and the City and cross the Thames at Tower Bridge.

**Judith** That's right. Cross that, the Tower of London is on the left and the World Trade Centre on the right and then, um, take the second right, there's a one-way system and then take the first left at the roundabout into Mansell Street and then the second left into Aldgate High Street.

**Debbie** ... into Old Gate High Street.

**Judith** No, Aldgate: A-L-D-G-A-T-E High Street. And then after the tube station, right and right again into **xxxxxx** Street and we're just on the left. There's an underground car park so there's no problem with parking.

**Debbie** Sorry, what was the name of the street again?

## Planning ahead

**1 Making plans**

We most often use the present progressive for plans made before the time of speaking:

I**'m meeting** Carlos for dinner tomorrow evening.
Next week I**'m visiting** a supplier in Warsaw.

It is also possible to use the verbs *plan* and *intend* in either the present simple or present progressive:

I **plan to** / **am planning to** have everything ready by June.
She **intends to** / **is intending to** return to work after she's had the baby.

 *Present progressive* page 12

**2 Making arrangements**

To speak about a definite arrangement for the future we can use *going to* + verb:

I'm **going to** go freelance shortly.
We**'re going to** talk about staffing levels at the next opportunity.

 *Future* page 28

**3 Talking about unfulfilled plans**

We use *mean to* or *want to* in the present perfect progressive when we have forgotten to do something we were planning to do or we have not had the chance to do it yet:

I**'ve been meaning to** get in touch with Katya but I haven't got round to it.
I know he**'s been wanting to** talk to you about it.

**4 Setting out to do something**

We use the expression *to set out to do something* when we decide to do something and make plans for it to be achieved:

We **set out** to be the number one player in the industry.
She **set out** with the intention of becoming chief executive.

**5 Describing arrangements**

We can use the future progressive to describe the plans and arrangements we have made:

I'm in Munich next week and I**'ll be seeing** Herr Röstel then.
When you're in London next month you**'ll be staying** at the Birkbeck Hotel.

For plans which we expect to be completed before a deadline we use the future perfect:

By this time next year we**'ll have completed** the reorganisation.

 *Future* page 28

## Practice

**A  Making arrangements**

A London-based consultancy called MarkUp is planning a seminar called *The Effective Global Manager*. The seminar organiser has received a copy of the provisional programme drawn up by a colleague who has made notes. Expand these notes into full questions.

| | |
|---|---|
| **Location** | Grosvenor House Hotel, Park Lane |
| **Date** | Monday 18–20 March |

**Provisional programme**                          *Which printer? No. of copies?* 1

**Sunday 17 March**
Delegates arrive at City Airport              *Transport?* 2        *Evening entertainment?* 3

**Monday 18 March**
Opening address                                      *Who?* 4
The changing business environment        Simon Kelly
Lunch

Cross-cultural communication                Pieter Oet
Communicating assertively                     Dwight Wayne
Cocktail and dinner                                *and then?* 5

**Tuesday 19 March**
Plenary session                                      Rod Weir      *Which room?* 6
                                                           *What subject?* 7

Re-engineering the corporation              Philip Price
Lunch                                                     *What about vegetarians?* 8
The learning manager                          Gavin Tudor
Workshops                                             Various – *how many rooms?* 9 *What size?* 10
                                                                        *equipment?* 11

**Wednesday 20 March**
Strategies, staff and systems                Lara Ford
Lunch

Financial skills                                       Michael Reynolds
Transfer to airport                                 *Time?* 12

Example:   *Who is going to print the programme?*
                   *How many copies will you be needing?*

## Reporting what people say or think (1)

**Form**   When reporting speech we can either use 'direct' speech or 'indirect' speech.

### 1  Using direct speech

We use the same words as the original speaker or reformulate them:

*Actual words:* 'We are not going to compromise with terrorists.'
*Report:* So then the Minister said, 'We are not going to compromise with terrorists.'

### 2  Using indirect speech

We make the speaker's words part of our sentence, changing verb forms and pronouns as necessary. It is not necessary to follow *said* by *that*.

The Minister said (that) **they were** not going to compromise with terrorists.

### 3  Reporting things just said

'Oh hello, Janet, Charles has just phoned and he **says** he **wants** to see you.'

The situation is still present.

### 4  Reporting things said in the past

We normally put the tense of the verbs originally used one tense back in the past if the original words were said some time ago:

| Original verb | Reported verb |
| --- | --- |
| 'I **don't** know how to cook an omelette.' | He said he **didn't** know how to cook an omelette. |
| 'She **is** getting annoyed.' | He said that she **was** getting annoyed. |
| 'I**'ve** forgotten the code.' | He said he **had** forgotten the code. |
| 'I**'ve been** trying to get through.' | She said she **had been** trying to get through. |
| 'They **will** never agree.' | She said they **would** never agree. |

If the original verb is already in the past tense, using the past perfect is optional:

'Martin **sent** them the invoice.'   She said that Martin (**had**) **sent** them the invoice.

### 5  Using modal verbs

Modal verbs do not change:

'You **could** / **might** / **should** go.'   She said that we **could** / **might** / **should** go.
'I **would** like to leave.'   He said he **would** like to leave.

## Practice

### A Reporting what the MD said

These are some of the things that the Managing Director said at a meeting you attended recently. A colleague who was unable to attend wants you to tell her what the MD said.

**1** 'I think a joint venture is the best way to break into the Middle East.'

.................................................................................................................

**2** 'We are not planning to set up a subsidiary.'

.................................................................................................................

**3** 'We've been talking to a group of investors in the Gulf.'

.................................................................................................................

**4** 'I've talked to the commercial attaché at the embassy.'

.................................................................................................................

**5** 'I don't want to diversify in the immediate future.'

.................................................................................................................

**6** 'We shouldn't attempt to move too fast because we might get our fingers burned.'

.................................................................................................................

**7** 'We will be sending Stuart Campbell on a fact-finding mission.'

.................................................................................................................

### B News in brief

Match the sentence halves in A and B.

**A**

**1** Richard Pound, the International Olympic Committee official leading the investigation into the corruption scandal engulfing the Olympic movement, said yesterday

**2** The director of the Office of Fair Trading said that car manufacturers

**3** The catering industry said that the new rules on genetically modified food

**4** The European Union's trade commissioner said that

**5** Britain and the US have told the United Nations

**B**

**a)** would be unenforceable and would put an unacceptable burden on food outlets.

**b)** the EU was prepared to put all its tariffs on the table for negotiation in the next round of talks.

**c)** were using recommended resale prices to mask the true selling price of vehicles.

**d)** to exclude their citizens from UN staff beginning to return to Afghanistan.

**e)** the IOC had been trying 'for years' to find proof that its members took bribes from bidding cities.

## Reporting what people say or think (2)

**Uses** 1 **Informing**

Would you like to **tell** her that she is being made redundant?

NL Industries **said** it **intended** to cut debt and increase capacity.

Indonesian police **told** reporters they were questioning three former central bank directors.

Note that *tell* and *told* are followed by an object (*tell her, told reporters*, etc.).

2 **Instructing**

I don't like autocratic bosses who **tell** employees **to work** harder.

She **told** him **to improve** his performance.

The court **told** the firm **to pay** £750,000 in compensation.

When *tell* and *told* are used in this way they are followed by an object + infinitive.

3 **Reporting the speaker's attitude and intention**

Note how the reporting verbs are used in the following extract:

Wim Duisenberg, president of the European Central Bank, yesterday **declared** the introduction of the euro a success. He **acknowledged** that Target, the new cross-border real-time payment system for the Eurozone, had had some teething troubles. But he **insisted** that all the main technical systems had coped well during last week's transition to the single currency.

He also forecast a potential conflict with European governments when he **warned** politicians against adopting an explicit exchange rate policy for the euro.

4 **Some reporting verbs are followed by an object + infinitive**

'If I were you I'd keep quiet.'          She **advised her colleague** to keep quiet.

'Don't sell your shares yet.'          He **warned me** not to sell my shares yet.

'Don't forget to take your passport.'          He **reminded her** to take her passport.

Others are followed by an infinitive:

'I'll send you a cheque.'          He **promised** to send her a cheque.

'We'll sue you if you cancel.'          They **threatened** to sue us if we cancelled.

'I'll give you a lift if you like.'          She **offered** to give me a lift.

Note that *suggest* and *recommend* are followed by two possible structures:

'You could hire more temporary staff.'          She **suggested** hir**ing** more temporary staff.

          She **suggested that** he **hire** more temporary staff.

## Practice

**A The minutes of a meeting**

Read this extract from a meeting and the minutes of the meeting. Choose the reporting verb which most accurately reflects what each speaker said.

| | |
|---|---|
| **Robert Dunne** | Right, let's start. The main item on the agenda is whether we reorganise our operations in France. I'd like to hear your views about this. Can you put us in the picture, John? |
| **John Marsh** | Yes. As you all know, we set up a regional centre in Lille two years ago. We hoped it would be a base for expansion into other areas of France and Benelux. Unfortunately, I have to say that it hasn't been a success. It hasn't made the kind of impact we expected and, as I see it, it's going to be very difficult to get much of a return on our investment. |
| **Robert Dunne** | Thank you, John. How do you feel about this, Gillian? |
| **Gillian Hall** | Well, if you remember I told everybody at the time that I was not in favour of Lille as a location. We should never have set up there. If you want to gain a foothold in the French market you've got to be in the capital. |
| **Robert Dunne** | Thank you, Gillian. What's your reaction, Mark? Do you think Gillian's right? |
| **Mark Atkins** | No, I don't agree at all. Benelux is a big market and Lille is right from a geographical point of view. I really think we need to give them more time. |
| **Gillian Hall** | Well, you've got a point, but what about the rest of France? You've got to be in Paris, like I said. |
| **Penny Mure** | I think the local staff are useless, they haven't done what they're employed to do. They never reply when I try to get in touch with them. |
| **Robert Dunne** | Is that true? |
| **Gillian Hall** | Yeah, that's happened to me on several occasions. |
| **John Marsh** | Look. Why don't we bring in a French consultancy to analyse the situation for us? We obviously need more information about what is going on. |
| **Robert Dunne** | OK, I'll look for a suitable firm of consultants in the next few days. If we don't do something quickly we'll just lose out to our competitors. |

> invited   pointed out   confirmed   disagreed   raised   reminded   advised
> warned   complained   outlined   suggested   offered   acknowledged

Mr Dunne ...................[1] the issue of operations in France and the siting of the regional centre in Lille and ...................[2] comments from the review committee. Mr Marsh ...................[3] the reasons for choosing Lille and ...................[4] that it had not been a success. Ms Hall .................[5] the meeting that she had never been in favour of Lille and ...................[6] that it was important to have a presence in Paris in order to gain a foothold in France. Mr Atkins ...................[7] and ...................[8] the committee to allow the Lille centre to continue for the time being. Ms Mure ...................[9] and Ms Hall ...................[10] that the staff in Lille were apparently incompetent. Mr Marsh ...................[11] that they hire a consultancy to investigate and Mr Dunne ...................[12] to look for a suitable firm and ...................[13] that there was a risk of losing market share if they didn't act swiftly.

## Reporting questions

**1  Reporting *yes/no* questions**

We use *if* or *whether* and make any necessary tense changes:

| | |
|---|---|
| '**Will** you be going to the reception?' | She asked me **if/whether** I **would** be going to the reception. |
| '**Did** you have a chance to speak to him?' | He wondered **if/whether** I **had had** a chance to speak to him. |

Note that there is no question mark in the reported question.

**2  Reporting open questions**

When questions begin with *which, what, where, why, when, how,* etc. we report them using a different word order:

| | |
|---|---|
| 'Where is the station?' | She wanted to know where the station was. (NOT *She wanted to know where was the station.) |
| 'When will you be leaving?' | He wondered when I would be leaving. (NOT *He wondered when would I be leaving.) |
| 'Which airline are you using?' | She asked me which airline I was using. |
| 'How much did you spend?' | He wanted to know how much we (had) spent. |
| 'Who told you?' | They wanted to know who (had) told me. |

The auxiliaries *do, does* and *did* are not used in the reported question:

| | |
|---|---|
| 'What time do you start?' | He asked me what time I started. (NOT *He asked me what time do I start.) |
| 'How much did it cost?' | He wanted to know how much it (had) cost. (NOT *He wanted to know how much did it cost.) |

We use a reported question after a phrase like *Do you know* or *Could you tell me* to request information:

**Do you know** how many people will attend?
**Could you tell me** if there is a phone box near here?
**Have you any idea** how much it costs? (NOT *Have you any idea how much does it cost?)

## Practice

**A** Sentence transformation

Report these *yes/no* questions using the words in brackets, as in the example:

**1** 'Do you want to call Derek?' (asked)

*He asked me if I wanted to call Derek.* ...............................................................

**2** 'Have you seen Bernard yet?' (asked)

........................................................................................................................

**3** 'Are you open on a Saturday?' (could)

........................................................................................................................

**4** 'Did you get my message?' (wondered)

........................................................................................................................

**5** 'How much time is there left?' (idea)

........................................................................................................................

**6** 'Will you be taking your husband with you?' (wanted to know)

........................................................................................................................

**B** Enquiries

Maria works at an information desk in an airport. These are the answers she gave – what do you think the questions were?

**1** The restaurant is upstairs.

*Someone asked her where the restaurant was.* ...........................................................

**2** 'You can get a shuttle outside the building.'

........................................................................................................................

**3** 'At the foreign exchange counter.'

........................................................................................................................

**4** 'The duty free is on the first floor.'

........................................................................................................................

**5** 'Yes, you can leave your suitcases in the left-luggage lockers over there.'

........................................................................................................................

**6** 'I'm sorry, I really don't know why the Alitalia flight has been delayed.'

........................................................................................................................

## Requesting and offering

**1 Making a request**

Here are some ways of making requests, according to the degree of politeness:

*impolite*

Get me another glass.   I want another glass.   Another glass, OK?

*neutral*

Can I have another glass, please?   I'd like another glass, please.   Is it all right if I have another glass?

*slightly more polite*

Could I have another glass, please?   May I have another glass, please?

*very polite*

I was wondering if I could have another glass.   Could you possibly give me another glass, please? Do you mind if I have another glass?   Would you mind my having another glass?

**2 Accepting a request**

Yes, sure.   Fine.   No problem.   Go ahead.   Certainly.

**3 Refusing a request**

I'm sorry, I can't. / That's not possible.   Well, I'm afraid … ( + reason)

If you want to refuse, you can say *Well, (actually) I'd rather not* (+ reason):

'Could you help me move this desk?' 'Sorry, I'd rather not. I've got a bad back.'

**4 Offering**

Would you like to …?   Would you like me to …?   Shall I …?

You can make a spontaneous offer using *I'll*:

'The last train has gone.' 'Don't worry. I'll give you a lift if you like.'

| *Accepting offers* | *Declining offers* |
|---|---|
| Thank you very much. | No, that's all right, thank you. |
| That's very kind of you. | No, don't bother. / I can manage. |

## Practice

**A Polite requests**

The following short dialogues are not very polite. Rewrite them to make them sound more acceptable.

Examples:    ~~I want to~~ speak to Mrs Gosso.

*Could I speak to Mrs Gosso, please?*

~~She isn't here. What do want to speak to her for?~~

*I'm afraid she isn't here. Would you like to leave a message?*

**1 A** I want to leave early.

   **B** No way.

**2 A** Want a lift?

   **B** Yes.

**3 A** Give me $50 until tomorrow.

   **B** I haven't got any money.

**4 A** Want a glass of sherry?

   **B** No.

**5 A** Bring me the bill.

   **B** OK.

**6 A** Tell me the way to the station.

   **B** No idea where it is.

**B Doing someone a favour**

Rearrange this jumbled dialogue between two colleagues and put these expressions into the blanks.

| could you possibly    I was wondering if    I'm afraid    go ahead    I'll    Shall I |
| --- |

**B** Well, ...............................[1] I can't tomorrow. I'm not coming in to the office.

**A** ...............................[2] write it down for you?

**B** Yeah, ...............................[3].

**A** ...............................[4] you could phone these people in Spain for me. My Spanish is atrocious.

**B** Sure. ...............................[5] do it first thing.

**B** Yes. Otherwise I'll forget! When do you want me to phone them?

**A** Well, ...............................[6] do it the day after tomorrow?

**A** Could I ask you a favour?

**B** No problem. Just tell me what you want me to say.

**A** Tomorrow.

## Suggesting

**1** *should* or *ought to*

You can use *should* or *ought to* to suggest what you think the right course of action is:

I think you **should** try a new strategy if the old one isn't working.
You **shouldn't** launch a new product without doing a market study first.
**Shouldn't** we ask him for his opinion?
They **ought to** simplify administrative procedures.
The government **ought to** reduce the rate of income tax.

Note that *oughtn't to* is possible but not very frequent.

**2** *could*

If you think it is possible to improve a situation and want to recommend a course of action you can use *could*:

We **could** reduce energy consumption by switching off PCs when they're not in use.
We **could** try to motivate staff by introducing a profit-sharing scheme.

**3** *shall we, let's, why don't we, how about, what about*

In the same way as *had better*, the forms *shall we, let's* and *why don't we* are not followed by *to*. *How about* and *what about* are followed by a verb + *-ing*:

**Shall we** offer them an increased discount?
**Let's** try to finish the meeting before 10 o'clock.
**Why don't we** lease equipment rather than buy it?
**How about / What about** leasing equipment rather than buying it?

**4** The verb *suggest*

Remember that the verb *suggest* is never followed by the infinitive. These are the correct structures. The words in brackets are optional.

I **suggest** that we (should) **get** some financial advice.
I **suggest** (our) **getting** some financial advice. (NOT *I suggest to get ...)

**5** *could always*

We say *could always* to suggest something that may solve a problem:

You **could always** review your reward system if you think people are losing motivation.

**Practice**

**A Making suggestions**

Match the problems with the proposed solutions. Complete the solutions using expressions from the box. (Be careful of the punctuation.)

> How about ...    Shall we ...    We could ...    Well, I suggest ...

1 We need to do something about our corporate image.

2 Her salary hasn't kept pace with the cost of living.

3 How are we going to get to the meeting at head office on time if there's a transport strike?

4 Where are we going to entertain the visitors while they're here?

5 Do you have any ideas on how to improve motivation?

a) ................... stay in a nearby hotel overnight?

b) ................... hiring a new public relations manager?

c) ................... taking them to a night club.

d) ................... give people more responsibility for decision-making.

e) ................... offering her some kind of promotion to a more highly-paid position?

**B Problem-solving**

Below are a number of problems. Make suggestions using language from the previous page.

1 We don't seem to be able to keep our skilled staff. They leave after two or three years and sell their services elsewhere.

2 Some of our customers are late in making payments and we have to send them a number of reminders before we get our money.

3 We'd like to get shelf space in the major supermarket chains but we haven't been able to do so.

4 Our firm seems to have a large number of old-fashioned computers and incompatible software. We don't know what to do with it all.

5 My boss gives me far too much work and doesn't seem to understand that I also have a family life.

MY BOSS GIVES ME FAR TOO MUCH WORK AND DOESN'T SEEM TO UNDERSTAND THAT I ALSO HAVE A FAMILY LIFE...

## Understanding signs and notices

**1 Giving information**

OUT OF ORDER: if a machine is not working
TO THE PLATFORMS: to direct passengers in a train station
SOLD OUT: if there are no goods left for sale
FOREIGN EXCHANGE COUNTER: in a bank; you can change currency here

**2 Asking people to do things**

PLEASE HAND IN YOUR KEY AT THE DESK: in a hotel lobby
EXACT FARE PLEASE: NO CHANGE GIVEN: on a bus
PLEASE PAY AT THE CHECKOUT: in a supermarket
PLEASE LEAVE YOUR TRAYS HERE: in a self-service restaurant

**3 Asking people not to do things**

KEEP OUT: Do not enter this property.
UNAUTHORISED VEHICLES STRICTLY FORBIDDEN: Do not park here.
DO NOT LEAVE BAGS UNATTENDED: Keep your bags with you.

**4 Warning**

MIND YOUR HEAD: The ceiling is low.
BEWARE OF PICKPOCKETS: Professional thieves may be around.
CROSS ONLY WHEN LIGHTS SHOW: or you may get run over.
WORKS ENTRANCE: The entrance to the factory is here.
TOLL AHEAD: You will have to pay to use this road / bridge / tunnel.
HEAVY PLANT CROSSING: Lorries, etc. come out of this entrance.

**Signs and notices**

Where would you see these signs and notices? Match them with the places below.

**a)** in a supermarket        **d)** in a car park     **g)** in a hotel

**b)** on a motorway        **e)** in an airport     **h)** in a filling station

**c)** on a box of laboratory equipment    **f)** in a bank     **i)** in a self-service restaurant

**1** FRAGILE

**2** Please pay at the Checkout

**3** Services 15 miles

**4** Self-service Please take a tray

**5** PAY AND DISPLAY

**6** THIS SIDE UP

**7** Please vacate your room by noon

**8** POSITION CLOSED

**9** PLEASE HAVE YOUR BOARDING PASS READY

**10** CHECK YOUR TYRE PRESSURE HERE

**11** The management cannot accept liability for guests' belongings left on the premises.

**12** DIVERSION AHEAD

**13** EXPRESS TILL: TEN ITEMS OR FEWER

# 15 Focusing on information

## Adding and combining information

**1 Adding information**

One simple way of adding extra information in writing is to separate it by dashes (−) or commas (,):

One of the goals of laser technology – a stable beam, blue laser operating at room temperature – is expected to be available for commercial use within six months. Nichia Chemical Industries, a small Japanese company, demonstrated a blue laser as early as 1993.

**2 Identifying people and things**

We use *who* or *that* to refer to people. To refer to things we use *which* or *that*:

The man **who** / **that** gave me my first job was a genius.
A modem is a device **that** / **which** sends information down the telephone lines.

To refer to places and time we use *where*:

Opposite is the National Gallery **where** you can see a lot of famous British paintings.

The clauses introduced by the relative pronouns identify and define the previous nouns. The pronouns are the *subject* of the relative clause and cannot be left out.

To refer to a time we use *when*:

A bank holiday is a day **when** most shops and offices close.

**3 Indicating possession**

If a person's credit card is stolen he / she should report it immediately.

Anyone **whose** credit card is stolen should report it immediately.

**4 Combining information**

Note how these two statements can be joined together into one sentence:

The group had a record turnover last year. The group is looking to continue its expansion.
The group, **which** had a record turnover last year, is looking to continue its expansion.

*Which* introduces extra, non-essential information and is said to be **non-defining**. *That* is not possible in sentences of this type. *Whose* can also be used to add further information:

Vendome, **whose** sales of prestige goods depend heavily on Japanese and east Asian consumers, has been hit by the turmoil in the region's economies.

## Practice

**A** Definitions: a financial quiz

Match the words to their definitions and provide a suitable relative pronoun (*that*, *which*, *where*, *who* or *whose*).

1 The over-the-counter market

2 Options

3 Floating exchange rates

4 Bears

5 A preference share

6 Names

7 A stock exchange

**a)** is a market ................... shares and government bonds are bought and sold.

**b)** are investors ................... believe share prices are likely to fall.

**c)** are wealthy individuals ................... provide funds to back Lloyd's insurance policies.

**d)** are financial instruments ................... give the right but not the obligation to buy or sell a commodity at a certain price.

**e)** is the market ................... securities are traded outside a regular exchange.

**f)** are the values of currencies ................... fluctuations against each other are set by market forces.

**g)** is a share ................... guarantees holders a prior claim on dividends.

**B** *Whose, who, which, that*

Complete each sentence appropriately.

1 The privatisation of Crédit Lyonnais, ................... final terms are soon to be decided, is expected to set the scene for the next step in the restructuring of the French banking sector.

2 Philip Coggan, ................... wrote *The Money Machine: How the City Works*, is a journalist with the *Financial Times*.

3 The BBC World Service, ................... is financed by the Foreign Office, said it intended to invest $14 million ($23 million) in improving its Internet services.

4 The product has been produced by a well-known company ................... perfumes have always been sold in the higher price ranges.

5 Ice cubes ................... crackle louder according to the strength of your drink have been developed in Japan.

6 We have developed a new computerised stock control system ................... will allow us to compete with our much larger rivals.

## Emphasising

**1 Using *so* and *such***

Certain words like *so, such, really* and *just* can be used to provide emphasis:

It is **so** much easier for men. They don't have to paint their nails for a meeting. (Eve Pollard, British journalist)

My boss is **such** a boring person. (NOT *a so boring person)

Our holiday was **really** / **just** fantastic.

**2 Using adjectives to provide emphasis**

You can stress your feelings about something by putting one of the following adjectives in front of a noun:

absolute   complete   entire   outright   perfect   positive   pure   real   total   true   utter   whole

For example:

The meeting was an **utter** waste of time, the chairman spent a **whole** hour talking **absolute** nonsense and any attempt to intervene was bound to be a **complete** failure.

**3 Adverbs used to provide emphasis**

The above adjectives can be transformed into adverbs by adding *-ly* (with the exception of *outright* which stays the same):

I was **absolutely** horrified.

I agree with you **entirely**.

The party was **truly** amazing.

He seems **perfectly** satisfied.

**4 Emphasising a statement**

If you want to emphasise the truth of an entire statement or stress its serious nature you can use the following words:

above all   actually   believe me   indeed   to put it mildly   to say the least

It was an unnecessary remark, **to say the least**.

**5 Emphasising a negative statement**

You can use *whatsoever* or *at all* after *none* or *no* + noun to focus on a negative statement:

There's **no** need **whatsoever** / **at all** to worry.

'Do you think he stands a chance of getting the job?' '**None whatsoever** / **at all**.'

**Practice**

**Ajaz Ahmed**

Complete the text using these words.

| whatsoever | to say the least | indeed | so | total | truly | whole | such |

Ajaz Ahmed is a ..................[1] remarkable man. He was recently voted the person who had made the biggest contribution to the development of e-business in Britain. This was, ..................[2], a tremendous achievement.

He left school at 16 and went to work at Dixons, the British retail chain selling electronic goods. At the age of 36, after being a store manager for much of his career, it became clear to him that Dixons should offer Internet access. It took him a ..................[3] three years to convince the board that the company should launch Freeserve, which, unlike other providers, offers access with no subscription cost ..................[4].

Freeserve has been a ..................[5] success and is likely to be floated off as a public company in its own right. Some say it may be worth over £2 billion. It took Stanley Kalms, the founder of Dixons, 40 years to achieve the same result. ..................[6], no one in Britain has ever before created ..................[7] much wealth in ..................[8] a short period of time.

## Expressing a reaction

### 1 Indicating your opinion

A number of adverbial expressions can be used to indicate your attitude to what you are talking about. They usually come at the beginning of the sentence and comment on the whole of it.

**In my opinion** we should never have accepted the work in the first place.
**Surprisingly** she accepted a decrease in salary without protesting.
I was once kidnapped in Afghanistan. **Luckily** I was released the same day.
**Ironically** his cold got better on the last day of his holiday.

They can, however, come after the verb *to be* like other adverbs:

**Predictably,** the Greens were opposed to the construction of a new power station.
The Greens were **predictably** opposed to the construction of a new power station.

The following adverbs are used to indicate attitude in this way:

absurdly admittedly coincidentally conveniently curiously fortunately incredibly interestingly mysteriously naturally oddly paradoxically sadly significantly typically unbelievably understandably unexpectedly unfortunately unhappily

### 2 Indicating your attitude

To make your attitude clear you can use:

| | |
|---|---|
| *in all* + abstract noun | e.g. **in all** sincerity / fairness |
| *to be (perfectly)* + adjective | e.g. **to be** (**perfectly**) honest / fair / frank |
| *to put it* + adverb | e.g. **to put it** mildly / crudely |

### 3 Exclamations

*What* + noun and *How* + adjective are used to make exclamations:

| | | |
|---|---|---|
| **What** a mess! | **What** a surprise! | **What** terrible weather! |
| **How** awful! | **How** amazing! | **How** nice of her! |

It is also possible to express reactions such as surprise, approval or disgust, etc. using exclamations or short phrases. These are some of the most common:

*approval:* Great! Superb! Mmm.
*disapproval:* Rubbish! Nonsense! What are you talking about?
*irritation:* Damn! Blast! For God's sake!
*surprise:* Wow! Gosh! You're joking!
*disgust:* Ugh! Yuk! That's ghastly!

## Practice

### A Indicating attitude

Complete the sentences using these words.

conveniently   mysteriously   typically   understandably   paradoxically

1 Decision-making .................... takes longer in cultures which are community-oriented and where there are sustained efforts to achieve a consensus. In individualistic cultures it is more acceptable to vote down those who disagree.

2 ...................., in ending welfare, the US may be committing itself to higher – rather than lower – levels of government support for the poor.

3 Mock job interviews are conducted at the beginning and end of each workshop. At the start, participants are .................... monosyllabic, hesitant, sometimes sullen. They mumble inaudibly when asked why they should be hired, often citing as justification the fact that they 'need a job'.

4 Strange things are happening in Westminster. Some clocks have started to go backwards and Big Ben has .................... stopped.

5 General Electric consists of 27 different businesses .................... grouped under one banner but managed separately.

### B Exclamations

1 Use *What, What a* or *How* to complete the exclamations.

1 .................... extravagant!

2 .................... mess!

3 .................... rubbish!

4 .................... awful!

5 .................... fantastic idea!

6 .................... disgusting!

7 .................... lucky!

2 React to these statements, using a suitable exclamation.

1 There are files all over the floor and piles of newspapers everywhere.

2 He spent half his monthly salary on clothes in just one day.

3 They eat the intestines of a sheep fried in fat and milk, with a chocolate sauce.

4 She won $1 million after buying her first lottery ticket ever.

5 Men and women can't possibly do the same kind of work.

6 He was going to be a pilot and then lost an eye in a road accident.

7 In polluted cities we could sell people fresh air in cans and make a fortune.

## Generalising / indicating relevance

**1 Generalising**

If you want to say that something is true, but maybe not 100% true, you can use a general introductory word or phrase:

**All in all** it has been a good year despite some uncertainties.
**Basically** the two machines are the same but with a different exterior.
**By and large** we treat our employees fairly.
**On the whole** we work together well even if we don't always agree.
**Overall** sales have been good, but not fantastic.

Other words used in this way include:

all things considered   as a rule   broadly speaking   for the most part
in general   on average   on balance   roughly speaking

**2 Indicating relevance**

If you want to state your field of reference you can use certain adverbs before an adjective or at the beginning or end of a clause:

**Technically,** glass-making is a relatively simple process.
It's not **politically** correct to say *fireman*; you should say *firefighter*.
**Aesthetically,** our head office is a very fine building.

It is also possible to use *from a / an* (adjective) *point of view*:

**From a financial point of view,** the idea doesn't make sense.
**From an ethical point of view,** hiring children would be wrong.

Some of these adverbs occur with *speaking*:

**Technically speaking,** 'England' only refers to one country, not the whole of the British Isles.
**Scientifically speaking,** matter is just packets of quanta.

From the *Financial Times*

**Practice**

**A** General statements

Make general statements from these prompts.

1 Charities, by ..................., are exempt from income tax.

2 All ................... it's been a pretty good year for our firm.

3 On ................... life was much less stressful in the past.

4 As ................... I try not to show favouritism to any of my staff.

5 In ................... about 10% of the candidates are offered positions.

**B** *... speaking*

Complete the following with one of these adverbs and *speaking*.

| broadly   relatively   technically   aesthetically |

1 ..................., the building is extremely ugly, even if it is functional.

2 ..................., bank managers belong to the middle class of society.

3 ..................., English is an SVO (subject, verb, object) language with a relatively fixed word order.

4 Humankind is, ..................., a newcomer on Earth.

**C** Points of view

The following sentences have been mixed up. Rewrite them so that they make sense.

1 From a military point of view, it is wrong to do to other people what you would not want done to you.

2 From an ethical point of view, Jupiter is an extremely interesting planet.

3 From an environmental point of view, it doesn't make sense to buy stocks when they've reached their peak.

4 From a scientific point of view, it is better to use aircraft to bomb strategic targets before using ground troops.

5 From a financial point of view, it is better to build on 'brownfield' rather than 'greenfield' sites.

## Highlighting information

### 1 Selecting

Some adverbs select a particular group of things or people from a larger set:

There is a substantial demand for employees in manufacturing, **notably** in electronics and telecommunications.

The group has £250m to spend on acquisitions and is looking **particularly** at Germany and the US.

Other adverbs used in this way include:

chiefly   especially   mainly   mostly   predominantly   primarily   principally   specifically

Some focusing adverbs point to one particular thing involved in what we are saying:

I was speaking to her **only** yesterday.
I was **just** / **simply** saying that she shouldn't be involved.
This offer is available **exclusively** / **solely** to our established clients.
Price **alone** is not a reliable indicator of quality.

### 2 Focusing on the topic

Clauses which have *what* as their subject focus on the thing you are talking about.

| Topic | Comment |
| --- | --- |
| What we need | is a bigger budget. |
| What impressed me most | was his professionalism. |
| What you have to do | is choose the right foreign partner. |
| What I would like | is a long holiday. |
| What I will do first | is give you a brief history of the project. |

### 3 Putting negative ideas first

When these expressions begin a sentence, the normal order of subject and auxiliary is reversed in order to emphasise the negative aspect:

**Never before** have we commissioned such an extensive survey.
**Under no circumstances** can we allow unauthorised visitors to enter the factory.
**On no account** should confidential information be shown to the press.

## Practice

**A Highlighting information**

Match the sentence halves.

| | | |
|---|---|---|
| **1** The population of Dublin is predominantly Irish, | | **a)** especially in urban areas. |
| **2** Her work as a pollster consists chiefly | | **b)** of interviewing members of the public. |
| **3** Violent crime is growing at a rapid rate, | | **c)** or, more specifically, Toledo. |
| **4** Boredom was mainly | | **d)** why I decided to quit. |
| **5** Some early doctors, notably Hippocrates, | | **e)** thought that diet and hygiene were important. |
| **6** Linda is hoping to move to Spain, | | **f)** but there are many other nationalities living there as well. |

**B Focusing on the topic**

**1** Change the focus of the topic in the following sentences, as in the example.

Example: I'm talking about a radical change in policy.

*What I'm talking about is a radical change in policy.*

**1** We need a good overseas partner.

**2** You have to have the right distribution network.

**3** You must make sure your products are suited to the local market.

**2** Francis Knight is giving a presentation. Here are three things he could say during his speech in order to focus on his intentions. Rewrite them, using *what*.

**1** I will first give you an idea of how the project started.

**2** I will then describe the project in more detail.

**3** I want to convince you that this project is worth investing in.

**C Negative ideas**

Rewrite these sentences in order to emphasise the negative aspect.

**1** We will never allow our firm to be taken over.

**2** You should under no circumstances handle dangerous products without protective clothing.

**3** You must on no account tell him about our plans.

## Linking (1)

We use link words, especially in formal writing, to signal the kind of connection there is between one statement and another.

These extracts show how some of the major link words are used to connect ideas which are contained in different sentences:

### 1 Contrast

Large-scale information technology projects are notoriously difficult to control. **However**, in the case of the massive euro conversion in 1999, everything went according to plan.

When a personal computer for home use is marketed strongly on the back of powerful visual images, the prospect of playing computer games becomes an important factor for many potential buyers. **Nevertheless**, it is difficult for manufacturers to establish just how far hardware sales are driven by game-playing.

Germany has been under pressure, especially from the United States, to plug legal loopholes which allow German businessmen to write off bribes abroad against tax.

**Yet** both Britain and even the United States, which has strict legal barriers against international bribery, are behind the Germans in intro

When we want to express a clear contrast between two subjects in the same sentence we can use *whereas*:

**Whereas** the traditional home PC used to be a stand-alone device, today's high-powered machines are designed to be multifunctional entertainment and communication devices equally capable of running the latest 3D adventure game, surfing the worldwide web for homework information or sending Granny an e-mail.

We use *although, in spite of* or *despite* before a statement that makes the main statement seem surprising or unlikely:

The results, **although** modest, were better than expected.

**Although** the currency crisis has hit local demand, the lower value of the baht has increased the competitiveness of exports.

**Despite** / **In spite of** advances in automated call technology, most people want to talk to a real person, not just a disembodied voice.

**Despite** be**ing** so unpopular, the present administration has successfully carried out a number of reforms.

## Practice

### A Contrasting

Underline the correct linking word in each of these paragraphs.

1 *Whereas /Although /Despite* having to wait four to five years before it is delivered to you, demand for a Stirling car is strong.

2 *Although /Despite /Nevertheless* American software firms are still well ahead of their European and Asian counterparts, the latter are catching up fast.

3 Demand and price go up and down, interest rates fluctuate, rival firms disrupt even the most carefully-laid plans, employees make mistakes. The list of potential disasters is long, that of opportunities much shorter. *In spite of /Yet /Despite* for most businesses the rules of the games and the types of disasters or opportunities stay much the same for years, or even decades, at a time.

4 *However /Although /Nevertheless* the types of jobs for which intercultural training is considered essential – namely expatriate positions – are on the decline, the globalisation of firms has increased the need for cultural sensitivity training.

5 Many women feel that full equality in the workplace has not been achieved. *Nevertheless /Although /Whereas* most will admit that there has been progress over the last 30 years.

6 *Whereas /Nevertheless /Despite* American companies are allowed to own 49% of a European airline, European groups are limited to 25% of US carriers.

### B Link words

Choose an appropriate linking word to connect these sentences.

1 ................... the issues were important, not many people bothered to vote.

2 There is no doubt that lowering interest rates early prevents recession. ..................., lowering them to cure a recession that already exists doesn't work.

3 ................... making a record profit last year, the firm has decided to lay off 500 employees.

4 Some cultures prefer meetings to start on time ................... others are not bothered about punctuality.

## Linking (2)

### 2 Result

If PC sales – and, **therefore**, sales of the Intel microprocessors which power most of them – are to continue to grow, the PC will need to 'win the battle for the consumer's eyeballs'.

There have been rumours of a take-over bid. **As a result**, the share price has soared.

The baggage-handling equipment often doesn't work properly. **Consequently**, baggage gets stuck on the conveyor system and the system breaks down.

### 3 Extra information

It's fast, comfortable and safe. It's very economical **too**.

Our firm has been investing heavily in getting more customers online. We've consulted clients widely on the design of our web pages and they have been improved over the past year. **In addition**, we have been running seminars to show our customers our services and how to make the most of them.

Advances in IT and in the globalisation of business have fostered the growth of knowledge-based companies and global brands. **Furthermore**, in many mega-mergers now, the main assets involved are often intangibles together with the resultant goodwill which often has a value of many billions of pounds.

### 4 Sequencing in time

Zimbabwe was **formerly** known as Rhodesia.
I'm really glad Barbara has found a job **at last**. She's been out of work for ages.
The plane **eventually** landed at 16.30, over four hours late.
The plane will be ready for take-off shortly. **Meanwhile** please wait in the departure lounge.
Many scientific theories were **subsequently** disproved by experimental evidence.

### 5 Ordering points

Sixty per cent of all business plans are rejected so it's important to bear in mind a few essential points if you're thinking of submitting a proposal to investors.

**First of all**, your plan must be factual yet attractive. **Secondly**, it must not be too long and it should not be repetitive. **Thirdly**, it should describe you, your business idea, what you need in the way of investment and what profit an investor may expect.

**Next**, you should describe the product or service. Explain the advantages. Is it cheaper? Is it better quality? What is its unique feature? **Then** you should describe your market, its future prospects and define your particular niche. **Last but not least**, you will need to provide financial forecasts for the next three years, including profit and loss accounts, cash flow statements and a specimen balance sheet.

## Practice

**A Categories of link words**

Organise these words under the headings.

| consequently  moreover  so  also  formerly  meanwhile  too |
| --- |
| subsequently  on the other hand  alternatively  eventually  thus |
| therefore  furthermore  even so  nevertheless |

| Contrast | Result | Extra information | Sequencing in time |
| --- | --- | --- | --- |
| .................. | .................. | .................. | .................. |
| .................. | .................. | .................. | .................. |
| .................. | .................. | .................. | .................. |
| .................. | .................. | .................. | .................. |

**B Link the statements**

Link the statements in column B with those in column A .

**A**

1  Heathrow is Europe's most modern airport.

2  I would like to spend more time with my family.

3  The drug has powerful side effects.

4  The weak demand for our products in the domestic market and in Asia hit us harder than we expected.

5  She's been under a lot of pressure recently.

6  I didn't enjoy the time I spent on the production line.

**B**

a) **Furthermore,** it may be addictive.

b) **However,** it is severely congested.

c) **Moreover,** competition in the US and Europe is increasing.

d) **On the other hand,** it did give me first-hand experience of factory work.

e) I have **therefore** decided to resign as chairman.

f) **As a result,** she's decided to take time off to relax a little.

## Substituting

**1**  *so*

To avoid repeating information we can use *so* and *not* after verbs such as *believe, hope, expect, guess, imagine, suppose* and *think*:

'Is Mr White in?' 'I think **so**.' (instead of repeating 'I think that he is in.')
'Will we lose money?' 'I hope **not**.' (instead of 'I hope that we will not lose money.')

We use *I'm afraid so* when we are sorry that the answer is *yes*:

'Will we lose money?' 'I'm afraid **so**.'

Negative sentences offer two alternative substitution structures:

'He won't change, will he?' 'No, I **don't** suppose **so**.' / 'No, I don't think **so**.'
'He won't change, will he?' 'No, I hope **not**.' / 'No, I'm afraid **not**.'

*Hope* and *afraid* are always used with the second structure (NOT *I don't hope so. / *I'm not afraid so.).

*I think **not**, I believe **not*** and *I suppose **not*** are a little more formal.

**2**  *such*

To refer back to a previously mentioned idea or statement we can use *such*:

The union wishes to introduce a 35-hour working week. I would oppose **such** a move.
'She wants to set up a utopian communist colony.' 'Where does she get **such** ideas?'

**3**  *this / that*

Both *this* and *that* can be used to refer back to something previously mentioned:

The key to meeting today's challenges depends more than ever on recruiting the right people. But **this / that** is easier said than done.

However, only *this* can point forward to something that hasn't yet been mentioned:

Good evening. **This** is the news.
**This** is the third time I've had to ask you when I will see the test results.

**4**  *the former / the latter*

When two items are presented in a list, it is possible to refer back to the first item using *the former* or the last-mentioned using *the latter*.

The Lexus and the Ferrari are luxury cars. **The former** is Japanese while **the latter** is Italian.

**Practice**

**A** *so* and *not*

Answer these questions positively using the words in brackets.

Example: Do you recognise this music? (think)  *Yes, I think so.*

1 Will he be able to take the initiative? (expect)
2 Will many people attend? (imagine)
3 Do you think he'll be angry? (guess)

Now react negatively.

Example: She won't want to leave late. (guess)  *No, I guess not.*

4 Will we be getting a bonus? (afraid)
5 It isn't dangerous, is it? (hope)
6 We'd better not use it without asking. (suppose)

**B** Avoiding repetition

Rewrite these sentences in order to avoid any repetition.

1 I may be free this afternoon. If I am free this afternoon, I'll come and see you.
2 Africa has long had a bad reputation for business – companies investing there fear the unknown, and often rightly fear the unknown.
3 A senior monetary official said that he regretted the decision not to join the EMU in 1999 for one particular reason. The operational structure of the Bank of England would have made a perfect role model for the European Central Bank – much more a perfect role model for the ECB than the German Bundesbank.

**C** Referring

What do the words in **bold** type refer to?

I propose setting up an International Credit Insurance Corporation as a sister institution to the IMF. **This new authority** would guarantee international loans for a modest fee. The borrowing countries would be obliged to provide data on all borrowings, public or private, insured or not. **This** would enable the authority to set a ceiling on the amounts it is willing to insure. Up to **those amounts** the countries concerned would be able to access international capital markets at prime rates. Beyond **these,** the creditors would have to beware.

The authority would base its judgement not only on the amount of credit outstanding, but also on the macroeconomic conditions in the countries concerned. **This** would render any excessive credit expansion unlikely. The capital of the proposed institution would consist of Special Drawing Rights. **This** would render its guarantees watertight. The SDRs would not be inflationary because they would be used only in case of default; at that time they would replace money that had been lost.

There are many issues to be resolved. The most important is the link between the borrowing countries and the borrowers within **those countries**. Special care must be taken not to give governments discretionary power over the allocation of credit because that could foster corrupt dictatorships. But once the need for **such an institution** is recognised, the details could be worked out. The institution can be set up only at a time when international lending is in a state of collapse. We are now entering **such a period**.

# Business communication skills

## Managing a conversation (1)

**1 Introducing a topic**

We very often use questions as an invitation to someone to develop a conversation. For example:

Did anyone see the film on television last night?
Have you heard about the change in plan?

We can also make an obvious statement such as:

You'll never guess what happened to me yesterday.

**2 Changing topic**

If you want to change the direction of a conversation you can say:

**By the way,** Jim phoned.
**While I think of it,** Jim phoned.
**While we're on the subject of** motivation, what kind of incentives do you offer?
**This is on a completely different subject,** but Jim phoned.

**3 Attentive listening**

When listening to another speaker, we usually react to what is being said by using various noises and expressions of encouragement and cooperation:

uh-huh   right   oh, really   oh dear   is that so?
yeah   mmm   I see   yes, of course   that's great

If we don't respond like this, we give the impression that we are not listening or are bored and the speaker may ask a question to check that we are following.

**4 Echoing**

Another way of showing that you are listening is to repeat a key word or phrase from what the other speaker has just said. For example:

**A** So, anyway, I said that I couldn't possibly accept 5%.
**B Five per cent?**
**A** Yeah, 5%, it's just not enough.

**A** ... and I was going to phone her before she got back from Japan.
**B Before she got back?**
**A** Yeah, because I needed a decision quickly.

**Practice**

**A Introducing a topic**

Introduce a topic of conversation that will elicit these answers.

1 ...............................................................................................

Yeah, she told me yesterday.

2 ...............................................................................................

No, I didn't, but I heard that it was very good.

3 ...............................................................................................

No, I haven't. What's happening?

4 ...............................................................................................

No. What went wrong?

**B Changing a topic**

You are in conversation and would like to change the topic. Write what you would say.

*Speech bubble (what you hear)*                              *Thought bubble (what you want to say)*

1

.... and so James went back and got the stuff that he'd forgotten and everything turned out OK.

Did James arrange for overtime at the weekend?

2

.... and I think that I'll probably have to go to China and see what's happening for myself.

Did you hear what happened in Beijing?

3

... and there seems to be a real change in spending patterns before the Christmas period, so we'll probably need to think about that.

Sandra wants to move into another section.

**C Echoing**

Unscramble these jumbled fragments of two conversations.

**A** And if you book before the end of the month you get a 10% reduction.
**C** Well, I thought there was something wrong with the system.
**A** Yeah, that's what it said on the leaflet.
**D** Something wrong?
**B** Before the end of the month?
**C** Yeah, but it was working all right in the morning.

## Managing a conversation (2)

5 **Following the conversation**

If we are having difficulty understanding, it is appropriate to ask for repetition or clarification:

Sorry, I don't quite follow you.     What was that again?

What was that you said about ...?     I didn't get that bit about ...

6 **Keeping going**

In conversation we need time to plan what we are going to say. In order not to hesitate too much and allow other people to intervene before we want them to, we use short expressions to gain thinking time:

Well, as I was saying ...     Anyway ...     I mean ...     And that's not all ...

So you see ...     And as you probably know ...

If we cannot think of a precise word and want to avoid hesitation, we use vague, imprecise language such as:

a kind of ...     a sort of ...     ... or something     it's a bit like a ...     ... and stuff like that

If we do not want to lose a turn, we use rising intonation to signal that we have not finished.

7 **Turn taking**

We sense that someone is about to finish what they are saying when they use falling intonation:

... and so I think we've got to move fast or we're going to lose out to the competition.

In more formal contexts, such as a meeting, it is possible to claim a turn by saying:

Sorry to interrupt but ...     If I may, I'd like to comment on that.

Excuse me ...     If I can just come in here ...

8 **Ending a conversation**

The end of a conversation has to be 'negotiated' so that no one is left talking:

'Well, I think that's all for now. I'd better be going.'

'Right. So, I'll see you on Wednesday, then.'

'OK. Yeah, Wednesday. Well, I'll let you get back to what you were doing.'

'Right. OK, Have a good trip.'

'Thanks. Bye.'

'Bye.'

**Practice**

A *sort of / kind of*

Look at the ways *sort of* and *kind of* are used in the following speech extracts. Match them with the approximate 'translations' (a, b or c) below.

1 ... and I think you know when some people are speaking English it's **kind of** like having a hot potato in your mouth ...

2 ... and if you didn't agree with him he got **kind of** angry.

3 ... er, no, it doesn't take that long to get authorisation, er, it's only **sort of** three or four months, I think.

4 ... and she didn't like living there and had a **kind of** nervous breakdown.

5 ... and Management by Objectives is a technique which has **sort of** gone out of date.

**a)** about

**b)** it seems

**c)** in a way

B Conversational acts

Match the words in bold with their functions (a–e) below.

1 It's not really good enough, **is it**?

2 **Sorry to interrupt**, but don't you think that's a little unreasonable?

3 'Shall we meet again next Monday?'

'Yes.'

**'Right.'**

4 ... and don't, **for heaven's sake**, believe everything you read in the press.

5 ... and he's got this thing about status and thinks that secretaries should be more than secretaries and **anyway** that's what he thinks. I think he sees them more as Personal Executive Assistants or something.

**a)** claiming a turn

**b)** stressing what the speaker himself says

**c)** keeping going

**d)** inviting feedback from the listener

**e)** acknowledging a response

## Negotiating

Negotiating involves a number of separate stages. Some useful language is given below for each stage.

### 1 Stating aims

What we need to decide is ...
Can we agree on an overall procedure?
We would like to reach agreement on ...
What we hope to achieve is ...
Let's establish some common ground.
We'd also like to discuss ....

### 2 Imposing conditions

We couldn't order that quantity **unless** you were prepared to ...
We can place a firm order only **on condition that** you pay within a week.
We can do business with you **provided that** you give us an open account.

 *Conditionals* page 34

### 3 Focusing the discussion

The key issue here is ...
One thing I want to look at is ...
What we need to talk about now is ...
We now come to the most important phase of our discussion.

### 4 Rejecting suggestions

That really isn't on.
I can't go along with that.
That's out of the question.
I'm afraid that's not acceptable.

### 4 Bargaining

**If** we give you extra discount **will** you increase the size of the order?
**If** you offered an extended guarantee we **could** see our way to reducing the price.
We might be able to make a concession **if** you **do** the same.

 *Conditionals* page 35

### 5 Summarising

Have I got this right?
We've agreed to ...
As we agreed, you will take care of ... and we will ...

If there are areas which you have not reached agreement on you can say:

There are one or two outstanding points / issues we still need to discuss.

### 6 Ending the negotiation

I think we've covered everything.
OK. It's a deal.
We can shake on that.

## Practice

**A** Negotiating an agreement

The government is encouraging firms to reduce the length of the working week in order to encourage job creation. But the implementation of a shorter working week is not easy and involves some tough bargaining.

The conversation below is the beginning of a negotiation between an employer and a union representative. Complete the dialogue by putting the missing extracts in the right position. (The dialogue reads diagonally.)

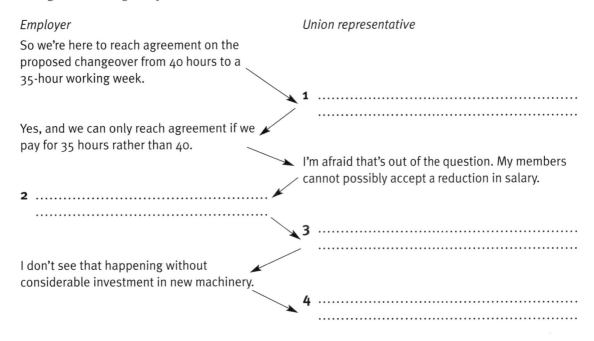

*Employer*

So we're here to reach agreement on the proposed changeover from 40 hours to a 35-hour working week.

**1** ...................................................................
...................................................................

Yes, and we can only reach agreement if we pay for 35 hours rather than 40.

I'm afraid that's out of the question. My members cannot possibly accept a reduction in salary.

**2** ...............................................................
...............................................

**3** ...............................................................
...............................................................

I don't see that happening without considerable investment in new machinery.

**4** ...............................................................
...............................................................

*Union representative*

---

**a)** Well, we seem to be getting nowhere. Let's see if we can establish some common ground.

**b)** That may be the case, but the company couldn't survive if we paid people the same wages for fewer hours.

**c)** I'm sorry, but I disagree. We can make productivity gains. If fewer people did the same amount of work in 35 hours there wouldn't be a problem.

**d)** Right, and the key issue is remuneration.

## Presenting figures

### 1 Whole numbers

We say *three hundred, six thousand, eight million*, etc. (There is no *s* at the end of these words.) BUT we add *s* for approximate numbers:

hundred**s of** people
million**s of** dollars, etc.

For figures over 100, British English, unlike American English, uses *and* between the hundreds and the tens:

327    BrE: three hundred **and** twenty-seven; AmE: three hundred twenty-seven
653    BrE: six hundred **and** fifty-three; AmE: six hundred fifty-three

We say *one thousand* rather than *a thousand* before a number of hundreds. The word *thousand* is not followed by *and* unless the figure is less than 1,100, 2,100, etc.

1,348    one thousand three hundred and forty-eight. (NOT *a thousand and three hundred)
1,001    one thousand and one
6,087    six thousand and eighty-seven

### 2 Decimals

If we have to use a decimal we say *point*. Each figure is said separately:

|  | 0.35 | 0.5 | 6.75 |
|---|---|---|---|
| BrE/AmE | zero point three five | zero point five | six point seven five |
| BrE | nought point three five<br>oh point three five | nought point five<br>oh point five | |

### 3 Fractions

Fractions are expressed using ordinal numbers:

a third    a quarter    a half    two-fifths    three-quarters, etc.

1:4 is pronounced *a ratio of one to four* or *one in four*.

### 4 Pronunciation

Many figures are pronounced individually:

A Boeing 757 (seven five seven)
Flight BA 316 (three one six)
Your code number is 4215 (four two one five)

When speaking about money, we say the currency unit after the figure if it is a whole number:

$75                seventy-five dollars
¥200,000,000    two hundred million yen
$75.50            seventy-five dollars fifty cents (*or* seventy-five dollars fifty)
€16.50            sixteen euros fifty cents

## Practice

**A Saying figures aloud**

Write down these figures the way they are said.

**1** 0.45 .........................................................................

**2** 1.85 .........................................................................

**3** $759 .........................................................................

**4** ¥125m .........................................................................

**5** 1/3 .........................................................................

**6** 2/5 .........................................................................

**7** 1:3 .........................................................................

**8** 2001 .........................................................................

**9** Your account number is 342 5461 .........................................................................

**10** Your personal identification number is 3749 .........................................................................

**B In your situation?**

Answer these questions.

**1** What proportion of your time do you spend in leisure activities?

**2** On average, how many children are born to each couple in your country?

**3** What is the average take-home pay in your country?

**4** What is the present rate of interest on a bank savings account?

**5** What is the rate of inflation in your country?

**6** What is the ratio of men to women at the workplace?

## Presenting information

The words and expressions below can be used for each of the stages involved in presenting factual or visual information. They are best learnt by heart as whole 'chunks'.

### 1 Introducing

The subject of my presentation is ...
What I'm going to talk about today is ...
I'd like to give you a brief overview of ...
The reason I am here today is to talk about ...

### 2 Structuring

I've divided my talk into (four) main sections ...
My presentation will be in (three) parts ...

First of all / Firstly   secondly   thirdly   then   after that   lastly / finally

### 3 Referring to visuals

As you can see from the table / pie chart / graph / diagram / flow chart / pictogram ...

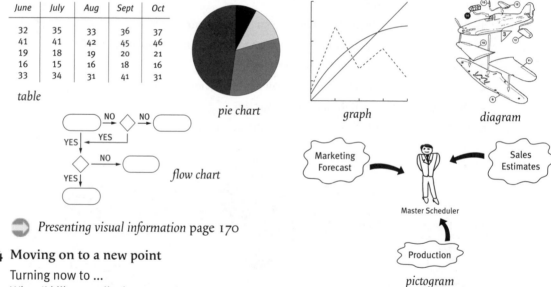

| June | July | Aug | Sept | Oct |
|------|------|-----|------|-----|
| 32 | 35 | 33 | 36 | 37 |
| 41 | 41 | 42 | 45 | 46 |
| 19 | 18 | 19 | 20 | 21 |
| 16 | 15 | 16 | 18 | 16 |
| 33 | 34 | 31 | 41 | 31 |

*table*

*pie chart*    *graph*    *diagram*

*flow chart*

Marketing Forecast    Sales Estimates    Master Scheduler    Production

*pictogram*

➡ *Presenting visual information* page 170

### 4 Moving on to a new point

Turning now to ...
What I'd like to talk about now is ...
Now I would like to describe ...
Now let's move on to the next point which is ...

### 5 Summarising and concluding

To sum up ...
To recapitulate what I've been saying ...
So, to go over the main points again ...
I'd like to conclude by saying ...

### 6 Ending a presentation

Thank you for listening to me.
If there are any questions, I'll be pleased to answer them.

## Practice

**A** Presenting a company

The text below is part of a presentation of a glass-making company. Fill in the blanks with the appropriate language.

---

firstly   Then   thirdly   secondly   If you look at   So to recapitulate   And to complete the picture
Now I would like to describe   As you can see from the transparency
I'd like first of all to give you an overview

---

- Good morning, ladies and gentlemen. .....................................................[1] of our company, Pilkington Glass.
- Pilkington is organised in three worldwide business lines. ...............................................[2], the Building products business, ...................................................[3] the Automotive products business and ...................................................[4] the Technical Glass products business.
- ...................................................[5] the Building products business accounts for about half the Group's sales and has manufacturing operations in 19 countries. Its largest operation is in Europe and we also have major operations in North and South America and Australasia.
- The Automotive products business represents around 45% of sales. Its organisation is sub-divided into two major units supplying original equipment and replacement glass. There are operations in 18 countries with a major presence in Europe and North America, and important operations in South America and Australasia.
- ...................................................[6] the Technical Glass products business accounts for the remaining sales and is centred in Germany, the United Kingdom, the United States and Italy. It manufactures glass for the electronic and optical industry, precision mirrors and solar energy panels.
  ...................................................[7] the company's structure. ...................................
  ...................................[8] the organisation chart, the various businesses report through their management boards to the chief executive. ...................................................[9], working from the corporate centre are Group functions – responsible for directing the businesses in their respective disciplines such as corporate affairs, environment and safety, finance, purchasing, legal and secretarial, human resources and internal audit. Technology is the only function that is organised centrally.
- That's all I want to say at this point on company structure.
  ...................................................[10], we have three major business lines, Building products, Automotive products and Technical Glass products. And there are various Group functions that report to the chief executive through the management boards. Are there any questions at this stage?

## Presenting visual information

### 1 Graphics

It is easy to produce tables, graphs, charts and diagrams to illustrate number-based information, thanks to word processing software and desktop publishing packages.

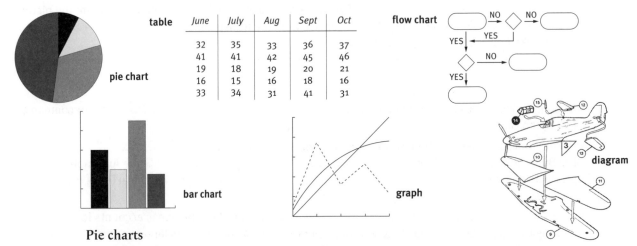

| table | June | July | Aug | Sept | Oct |
|-------|------|------|-----|------|-----|
| | 32 | 35 | 33 | 36 | 37 |
| | 41 | 41 | 42 | 45 | 46 |
| | 19 | 18 | 19 | 20 | 21 |
| | 16 | 15 | 16 | 18 | 16 |
| | 33 | 34 | 31 | 41 | 31 |

### Pie charts

A pie chart has good visual impact but does not show movement:

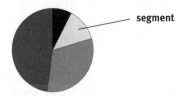


### Bar charts

Bar charts can be presented vertically or horizontally. They are particularly good for making comparisons:

### Tables

Tables give very precise information, but their visual impact is very poor and they should be avoided during presentations as they may be difficult to read:

**TOURIST RATES**

| | |
|---|---|
| Australia ($) | 2.4153 |
| Austria (schillings) | 20.60 |
| Belgium (francs) | 60.55 |
| Canada ($) | 2.3658 |
| Cyprus (pounds) | 0.8646 |
| Denmark (krone) | 11.21 |
| Finland (markka) | 8.9379 |
| France (francs) | 9.8273 |
| Germany (marks) | 2.9390 |
| Greece (drachma) | 493.67 |
| Hong Kong ($) | 12.46 |

### Flow charts

Flow charts are used to illustrate the stages in a process. The branches show when a decision has to be made:

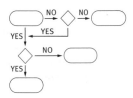

### Graphs

Graphs are good for showing movements and how one thing varies against another:

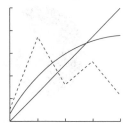

### Diagrams

A diagram is an illustration designed to show how a machine or system functions:

## 2  Describing a graph

It is not necessary to describe every single movement on a graph; an outline of the main trends is enough:

This graph shows world gross domestic product growth from 1973 until the end of the 20th century. With the oil crisis in 1973, GDP growth fell sharply by 5%, from 7% in 1973 to 2% at the end of 1975. It recovered in the following year before declining ever further in the next six years to reach a low point of 1% in 1982. Over the next two years GDP growth rose steadily to reach 5% but fluctuated in the following years before plummeting again in 1997. It reached a low point of 1.5% before edging up slightly in 1998–99.

% increased on year

**World GDP growth**

Intransitive verbs of movement:

| up | down |
|---|---|
| to rise | to fall |
| to rocket | to plummet / to slump |
| to edge up | to dip |
| to pick up | to go down (NOT *to pick down) |
| to grow / recover | to decline |

Note: Some verbs are transitive and need an object. For example:

to raise (prices, taxes)
to boost (the economy, sales)

**Practice**

## A Illustrations

Label the following visuals with these words:

> bar chart   curve   diagram   dotted line   flow chart
> graph   horizontal axis   pie chart   table   vertical axis

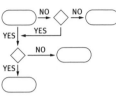

............................. 1

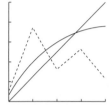

............................. 2

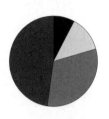

............................. 3

............................. 4

| June | July | Aug | Sept | Oct |
|------|------|-----|------|-----|
| 32 | 35 | 33 | 36 | 37 |
| 41 | 41 | 42 | 45 | 46 |
| 19 | 18 | 19 | 20 | 21 |
| 16 | 15 | 16 | 18 | 16 |
| 33 | 34 | 31 | 41 | 31 |

............................. 5

............................. 6

............................. 7

............................. 9

............................. 10

............................. 8

## B Describing graphs

**1** Complete the paragraph with these prepositions.

> of   to   by   at   under   from

At the end of April, sales stood ..................¹ $150 million, having risen ..................² a previous low point ..................³ just ..................⁴ $100 million . Over the next couple of months they rose steadily to reach a peak ..................⁵ $190 million. They then fell sharply ..................⁶ $35 million towards the end of July, but crept up again in August ..................⁷ $160 million.

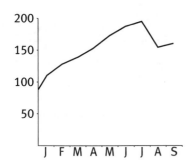

**2** Write three short paragraphs to accompany these graphs which describe three of Japan's economic indicators.

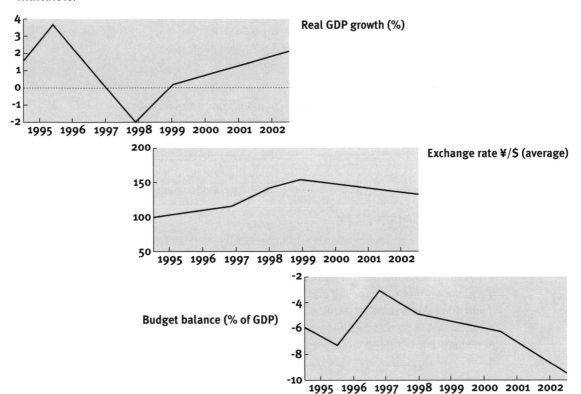

Real GDP growth (%)

Exchange rate ¥/$ (average)

Budget balance (% of GDP)

## Social interaction

**1 Saying hello**

*to friends*: Hi!   Hello!   Morning!   How're you doing?
*in more formal situations*: Good morning. Good afternoon. Good evening.

Note: Only say *Goodnight* if you are saying goodbye in the evening.

**2 Introducing yourself**

My name's ...
I'm ...
Let me introduce myself. My name is ... (more formal)

**3 Introducing others**

This is ...
I'd like you to meet ...
Do you know ...?
Have you met ...?

If you are introduced to someone who says *How do you do?* the response is *How do you do?*

**4 Polite responses**

**Saying thank you**

It is best to reply when someone thanks you for doing something or giving something.

| *Thanks* | *Possible response* |
|---|---|
| You've been very helpful. | Don't mention it. |
| I appreciate your help. | My pleasure. |
| Thank you for your help. | You're welcome. |
| Thanks for the ride. | Any time. |

**Saying goodbye**

| *To a friend* | *In more formal situations* |
|---|---|
| I'd better be going. See you. | I'm afraid I have to leave now. |
| See you later / soon / some time. | I must be on my way. |
| Take care. | It was very pleasant meeting you. |
| All the best. | Enjoy the rest of your stay. |
| Mind how you go. | I look forward to seeing you again. |

**5 Reacting to what people say**

You can use the following words and expressions in these situations:

*when you don't hear something clearly*:  Sorry, I didn't catch that.
*when you think something is fantastic*:  Wow!
*if you think something doesn't matter very much*:  Never mind.
*if you don't understand something*:  How come?
*when someone says something you find difficult to believe*:  You're joking!
*to compliment or offer good wishes to someone*:  Congratulations!

**Practice**

## A Reacting to what people say

Match these expressions with the thoughts behind them (1–5). Then use the expressions to respond to sentences (a–e).

| Oh dear!   I didn't quite catch that.   Never mind.   How come?   You're joking! |

**1** ◯ That seems absurd.

**2** ◯ I didn't understand what you just said.

**3** ◯ I don't understand how this thing happened.

**4** ◯ It doesn't matter; it's not terribly important.

**5** ◯ I sympathise with you.

**a)** And the deal fell through even though we were 100% sure of getting the order.
..............................................

**b)** I think I've erased your file.
.................. I've got a backup copy.

**c)** Well, I suggest we invite the President of the United States to open the new canteen.
..............................................

**d)** I think I've erased my file and I haven't got a backup copy.
..............................................

**e)** Cantchergettertedoitnow?
..............................................

## B Conversational pairs

Match the sentence on the left with the response on the right.

| | |
|---|---|
| **1** I'm getting married in the spring. | **a)** It was my pleasure. |
| **2** Thanks for the ride. | **b)** Fine, thanks. |
| **3** How do you do? | **c)** Wow! |
| **4** How're you doing? | **d)** No, it's true, I assure you. |
| **5** I'll get another round of drinks. | **e)** Yeah, take care. |
| **6** Thank you for a wonderful time. | **f)** No, this one's on me. |
| **7** Here's to a successful partnership! | **g)** Any time. |
| **8** We made over a million bucks in five days. | **h)** How do you do? |
| **9** You're joking! | **i)** Congratulations. |
| **10** Bye then. | **j)** Cheers! |

## Taking part in meetings

Some common expressions used in meetings are given below.

**1 Opening a meeting**

Thank you for coming.
Let's make a start, shall we?
Shall we begin?

You've all received a copy of the agenda.
The first item on the agenda is ...
James, would you like to start?

**2 Stating the purpose of a meeting**

The aim of this meeting is to discuss ...
What we are here to talk about is ...
We need to reach a decision on ...

**3 Beginning the discussion**

The first point that needs mentioning is ...
If I can just fill you in with the background to this ...

**4 Calling on a speaker**

Would anyone like to comment?
Paula, what do you feel?

I'd like to ask Dennis for his view.
Janet, do you have anything to add at this point?

**5 Moving on to another topic**

I'd like now to move on to ...
The next item on the agenda is ...

Can we go on to think about ...?
The next thing we have to discuss is ...

**6 Checking everyone agrees**

Do we all agree?
Is that unanimous?

Are we all happy about that?
Is that decided then?

**7 Summarising decisions taken**

So what I think we've said is that ...
To recap ...
So to sum up ...

**8 Concluding the meeting**

Is there any other business?
I think we've covered everything.
That's it then.

I declare the meeting closed.
That brings the meeting to a close.

*Is that unanimouus?*

## Practice

**A Chairing a meeting**

Match the functions (1–8) with the way they can be expressed (a–h).

1 opening a meeting
2 stating the purpose of a meeting
3 beginning the discussion
4 moving on to another topic
5 checking everyone agrees
6 concluding the meeting
7 summarising decisions taken
8 calling on a speaker

a) Let's move on to the next item on the agenda.
b) Perhaps Mrs Beck can tell us something about …
c) So, what we've decided today is to …
d) Shall we make a start?
e) Thank you for coming and for your contributions.
f) Is that to everybody's satisfaction?
g) We're here today to talk about …
h) I'd like you in turn to give your points of view.

**B Taking part in a meeting**

Match the functions (1–6) with the way they can be expressed (a–f).

1 interrupting someone
2 making a point strongly
3 asking for clarification
4 agreeing
5 disagreeing
6 expressing a doubt

a) Sorry, I don't quite follow you. Could you be more specific?
b) I'm not entirely sure that …
c) That suits me fine.
d) I'm afraid I can't go along with that.
e) I *do* think it's important to …
f) If I could just come in here.

## Telephoning

### 1 Answering the phone

The person who answers the phone always starts the conversation.

In formal or business situations you usually give your name or the name of the company:

Hello, Mary Wells speaking.
Good morning. IKI Industries. How may I help you?

### 2 Stating the reason for a call

Hello. My name's …
I'm ringing to …
I'm ringing about …
I'm phoning because …

### 3 Leaving and taking messages

Can I leave him a message?
Can I give him a message?
I'll pass that on to her.
Could you ask her to get back to me?

### 4 Asking for repetition

Sorry, I didn't quite catch that.
Could you repeat that, please?
Could you speak up a little?

### 5 Taking down addresses and telephone numbers

When writing or dictating an address you need to know how to pronounce the letters of the alphabet. The individual letters are pronounced with the same vowel sound as the words on the left.

| | |
|---|---|
| sp**ea**k /iː/ | B, C, D, E, G, P, T, V, Z (pronounced *zee* in American English) |
| t**e**ll /e/ | F, L, M, N, S, X, Z (pronounced *zed* in British English) |
| w**ai**t /eɪ/ | A, H, J, K |
| thr**ough** /uː/ | Q, U, W |
| ph**o**ne /əʊ/ | O |
| l**i**ne /aɪ/ | I, Y |
| c**a**rd /ɑː/ | R |

Telephone numbers are pronounced in groups. The groups usually correspond to a particular coding system. The digits are said separately, but a repeated number can be said as *double x*. For example:

| double zero | three one | seven zero three five | double four six seven eight |
|---|---|---|---|
| 00 | 31 | 7035 | 44678 |
| International | the Netherlands | The Hague | the number |

### 6 Ending a call

*informal:* Thanks for your call. Bye now.
*formal:* Thank you for your call. / Thank you very much. Goodbye.

**Practice**

**A  A phone conversation**

Number this jumbled conversation in the correct order. The first one has been done for you.

..... I'll sign them this afternoon and send them back to you.

..... Hello. My name's Beata Szlachetka. I'd like to speak to Katie Chapman, please.

..*1*.. Good morning. IKI Industries. How may I help you?

..... Hold the line, please. I'll see if she's in.

..... Great. Thanks a lot.

..... (pause) Hello. Katie Chapman speaking.

..... Beata Szlachetka and I'd like to speak to Katie Chapman.

..... Hello, this is Beata.

..... Sorry, I didn't quite catch that.

..... Hi, Beata. How are you doing?

..... OK. Busy as usual.

..... Fine, thanks. And you?

..... Yeah, they came this morning but I haven't signed them yet.

..... I'm just ringing to find out if you've received the copies of the contract.

..... OK, there's no rush.

**B  Telephone language**

Look at these expressions which are often heard or used when telephoning. Decide which are from recorded messages, and mark them with X.

1  Sorry to keep you waiting.

2  Pearson Travel. Christine speaking. How may I help you?

3  I'll get him to call you back as soon as possible.

4  Hold on a moment and I'll put you through.

5  Could you put me through to the accounts department, please?

6  Could you speak up a little?

7  We are unable to take your call at the present time. Please leave your name and number after the tone.

8  This is the Australian Embassy visa information line. The consulate section is open every morning from 10 o'clock to 1 o'clock.

**C  Taking someone's name**

Write the names of the people in the blanks.

1  My name's ...........................; I'll spell that for you – gee are ay aitch ay em new word aitch you gee aitch ee es.

2  My name's .........................: that's jay eh en i see ee new word why oh you en gee.

# Answer key

## Present simple (1)

**A** Mission statements

**1** welcome   **2** spend   **3** lead   **4** come   **5** means   **6** depends   **7** introduce
**8** improve   **9** work   **10** stay   **11** enables   **12** delivers   **13** strive   **14** cultivates
**15** endeavours   **16** acknowledges   **17** gives   **18** fosters   **19** help

**B** General truths

**1** buy; put   **2** talks; say   **3** means   **4** promise   **5** tends   **6** believe; believe

## Present simple (2)

**A** A travel booking

**1** need   **2** starts   **3** Do ... want   **4** depends   **5** does ... cost   **6** is   **7** gets   **8** takes
**9** leaves   **10** arrives   **11** do ... have to   **12** do ... make

**B** A summary of a report

**1** focuses   **2** highlights   **3** provides   **4** recommends   **5** calls for

**C** Headlines

**1** f   **2** e   **3** a   **4** c   **5** b   **6** d

## Present progressive (1)

**A** Events in progress

*Specimen answers*

**1** A man is typing on a laptop.

**2** A film crew is making a documentary.

**3** Some people are working in a factory.

**4** A woman is welcoming a visitor.

**5** A woman is making a presentation

**6** A man is buying something / paying for something with a credit card.

**B** News in brief

**1** d   **2** b   **3** a   **4** e   **5** c

**C** Temporary situations

*Specimen answers*

**1** ... more people are using their cars.

**2** ... she's having to deal with a lot of extra work.

**3** ... we're living in a bit of a mess.

**4** ... I'm changing all my money into dollars.

## Present progressive (2)

**A** Changes

*Specimen answers*

**1** The government is taxing companies that pollute the environment.

**2** The government is putting up the rate of income tax.

**3** The government is changing the law relating to working conditions.

**4** The minister of transport is inaugurating a new underground line.

**5** The government is closing down schools.

**6** The government is building more hospitals.

**B** Arrangements

*Specimen answers*

**1** 'm visiting our London office.

**2** 'm seeing a new customer

**3** 'm not doing anything special.

**C** Present simple or present progressive?

**1** regular activities PS

**2** temporary situations PP

**3** fixed timetables PS

**4** giving instructions PS

**5** an event in progress PP

**6** permanent and factual situations PS

**7** a present arrangement for the future PP

**8** mental states PS

**9** trends and changing situations PP

**10** doing by saying PS

**a)** 2 **b)** 3/6 **c)** 5 **d)** 7 **e)** 6 **f)** 10 **g)** 8 **h)** 4 **i)** 9 **j)** 1

## Unit 2

## Past simple

**A** Important firsts

**2** The Wright brothers made the first flight in 1903.

**3** Neil Armstrong landed on the surface of the moon in 1969.

**4** Pierre and Marie Curie discovered radium in 1902.

**5** Gutenberg invented the printing press in 1434.

**6** Isaac Singer patented the first commercial sewing machine in 1851.

**B The Bell story**

**1** began   **2** introduced   **3** said   **4** opened   **5** had   **6** went   **7** employed
**8** amounted   **9** decided   **10** ran   **11** offered   **12** launched   **13** set up   **14** totalled

**C An annual report**

**1** improved   **2** made   **3** hindered   **4** chose   **5** gave

**A The reasons why**

# Past progressive

**2** They evacuated the building because the fire bell was ringing.

**3** He sold his shares quickly because their value was plummeting.

**4** He didn't wish to interrupt because the president was speaking.

**5** I cut down on drinking because my work was suffering.

**6** We were forced to withdraw the model because customers were complaining.

**B Steve Jobs**

**1** d)   **2** c)   **3** a)   **4** b)

**A Susan George's CV**

# Past perfect simple

**1** had obtained   **2** had spent   **3** had been   **4** had developed   **5** had marketed

**B Regrets**

**1** had got   **2** had obtained   **3** had done   **4** had lasted

# Past perfect progressive

**A Previous and subsequent events**

**1** had been; had been waiting

**2** had been working

**3** had seen; had not impressed

**4** had been falling

**5** had been hiding

**6** had been stealing

**7** had been looking

**B** Marcel Bich

1 had created

2 had studied / had been studying

3 had been selling

4 had studied / had been studying

5 had been working

## Unit 3

### Present prefect simple (1)

**A** Stella McCartney

1 has taken    2 was    3 has transformed    4 has increased    5 hasn't seen    6 took
7 was    8 was    9 knew    10 had    11 has stuck    12 has kept

**B** Market news in brief

1 has agreed    2 have slumped    3 issued    4 gave    5 has bought

### Present perfect simple (2)

**A** Previous experience

1 Has he ever been in charge of a team?

Yes, he was in charge of a team at Steelcase Strafor.

2 Has he ever set up a business?

Yes, he set up an import company between 1997 and 1999.

3 Has he ever had direct sales experience?

No he hasn't, but he has planned roadshows for the launch of new products.

4 Has he ever used Excel?

Maybe, because he has used Microsoft Office.

5 Has he ever organised exhibitions?

No he hasn't, but he has organised roadshows.

6 Has he ever dealt with export procedures?

Yes, he has dealt with customs clearance.

**B** Time words

| *Used with the present perfect* | *Used with the past simple* |
| --- | --- |
| since | ago |
| yet | yesterday |
| so far | at 3 o'clock |
| over the last two years | during the 1990s |
| lately | last year |
| for the past three weeks | |

1 already    2 over the past three years    3 two years ago

## Present perfect progressive

**A** Recent activities

*Specimen answers*

**1** I've been working on a new database.

**2** I've been working with a team of consultants.

**3** I've been trying to find a house nearer to my place of work.

**B** The effects of recent events

**1**

**b)** Some members of staff have been stealing them.

**c)** Someone has been leaking information to the press.

**d)** The chemicals plant has been discharging waste into the river.

**e)** She's been having Spanish lessons.

**2**

**a)** How long have you been waiting?

**b)** I've played tennis four times this week.

**c)** Look outside. It's been raining; the pavement's still wet.

**d)** 'You look tired'. 'I've been driving all day long'.

**e)** I've known John since we were at school together.

**f)** The government has announced a drop in unemployment.

**g)** I've been reading a book on negotiating skills but I don't think I'll finish it.

**h)** He's been working as a consultant for three different firms in the same sector of activity; I think there's a conflict of interest and he should resign.

**i)** He has worked as a consultant for three different firms in the same sector of activity, but was fired from the first two.

### Unit 4

## Future (1)

**A** Ambitions

**1** Susan is going to be a pilot.

**2** Linda is going to be a racing driver.

**3** Elizabeth is going to be a doctor.

**4** Michael is going to be a policeman.

**5** Kevin is going to be an astronaut.

**6** Sean is going to be a disk jockey.

**B** Predictions

**1** c   **2** d   **3** b   **4** a

# Future (2)

**A** Making offers

1 I'll open a window.

2 I'll have a look at it for you.

3 I'll give you a hand.

4 I'll give you a lift.

5 I'll help you do them if you like.

**B** Schedules

1 What time does flight No. BA3287 arrive in Birmingham?

2 How long does the flight from London to Manchester take?

**C** Future perfect or future progressive?

1 By 2020 the first men will have landed on the planet Mars.

2 In the next hundred years, the Netherlands will have disappeared under water.

3 In the second decade of the 21st century people will be eating more genetically modified food.

4 By 2030 Chinese will have become the language of international scientific communication.

5 Many people will be living to over 100 as medical science advances.

# Future (3)

**A** Travel arrangements

1 will be staying

2 will be exploring

3 visiting

4 will be taking

5 will be visiting

6 will be returning

7 transferring

**B** *if, when, until, as soon as*

1 I'll get / I'll be getting in touch when I return from the Middle East.

2 If they shut down the plant, a lot of people will lose / will be losing their jobs.

3 We won't start until everyone is here.

4 He can't make a decision until he sees the president.

5 A project to create a bacterial cell from inanimate chemicals will go / will be going / is to go ahead as soon as it receives / has received approval from an ethics committee.

**C** Announcements

1 MICROSOFT TO IMPROVE WEBSITE

2 BMW TO REPLACE ROVER MODELS

## Unit 5

### Conditionals (1)

**A** It's generally the case

**1** f  **2** e  **3** b  **4** c  **5** g  **6** d  **7** a

**B** Future consequences

*Specimen answers*

**1** If my car is stolen, I will report it to the police.

**2** If a close colleague gets married, I'll buy him a wedding present.

**3** If I am offered a better-paid job abroad, I may accept.

**4** If my firm is taken over by a competitor, I may be moved to another department.

**5** If I have to give a presentation in English, I'll ask my English teacher for help.

**6** If my computer is infected with a virus, I'll call an expert for assistance.

**C** *if / unless*

**1** If  **2** unless  **3** If  **4** If  **5** Unless  **6** unless  **7** if  **8** If

### Conditionals (2)

**A** Imagining

*Specimen answers*

**1** If the world was governed by a Communist superpower people would not have the same freedom.

**2** If my husband/wife was offered a good position in Iceland I would probably refuse to go.

**3** If I stood for the presidential elections I wouldn't get through the first round.

**4** If the sale of alcohol was banned in Europe there would be fewer road accidents.

**5** If I were accused of selling my country's military secrets I would be sent to prison pending trial.

**B** Bargaining

**2** If you give me a special price I'll put in a bigger order.

**3** I'll take last year's stock if you take off 15%.

**4** I'll purchase the equipment if you throw in the accessories.

**5** How long will you hold your prices if we order today?

**6** If I pay cash how much discount will you allow?

**C** Negotiating positions

**2** If we made a firm order would you agree to split the transport costs 50–50?

**3** If we ensured free maintenance would you buy a new photocopier from us?

**4** If I bought the turbo-diesel model would you install air conditioning and a CD-player free of charge?

**D** *provided (that), so long as, on condition (that)*

*Specimen answers*

**1** I agree to work seven days a week on condition that I'm paid treble time for the weekend.

**2** I agree to take a cut in salary provided that I have less work to do.

**3** We agree to make a special delivery so long as it's not on a Sunday.

## Conditionals (3)

**A** A negotiation breakdown

*Specimen answers*

If I had been John Dee I would not have walked out of the discussion. I might have stayed later.

If I had been Mrs Han I would have made some sort of offer for him to consider as a compromise solution.

**B** Sola-Soda

*Specimen answer*

If I had been director-general of Sola-Soda Enterprises I would have called a press conference and tried to restore consumer confidence.

**C** Mixed conditionals

**1 a)** yes    **b)** yes

**2 a)** no    **b)** no

**3 c)** yes    **d)** no

**4 c)** no    **d)** yes

## Unit 6

## Verb + verb + *-ing*

Verb + verb + *-ing*

**1**

**1** e    **2** a    **3** d    **4** c    **5** b

**2**

**a)** I don't mind travelling as long as there are no delays.

**b)** My job involves meeting many people.

**c)** I firmly deny passing on any trade secrets.

**d)** We risk losing business to our competitors.

**e)** She suggests getting in touch with the commercial attaché.

**f)** We fully anticipate doubling our turnover in the next two years.

**g)** He was late so I missed seeing him.

**h)** How can you justify spending so much on entertainment?

## Verb + *to*-infinitive

**A** Verb + *to*-infinitive

1  I fully intend to complain.
2  Please remember to send them the samples they requested.
3  We undertake to provide a 24-hour-a-day hot line.
4  I expect to receive an answer soon
5  They have offered to send a replacement.
6  She neglected to tell them of the potential problem.
7  There appears to be a bug in the program.
8  She claims to have the necessary authority.

## Verb + object + *to*-infinitive

**B** Verb + object + *to*-infinitive

1  She taught me to believe in myself.
2  They paid me to do their dirty work.
3  He programmed the robot to perform a certain number of tasks.
4  The employers' federation urged the Minister to cut interest rates.
5  The joint venture enabled us to benefit from our partner's expertise.

## Verb + object + verb + *-ing*

**A** Verbs of perception

1  moving    2  coming    3  beating    4  having    5  feeling    6  lying    7  whispering
8  going through    9  shout

**B** Verb patterns

1  I find it impossible to work with him.
2  They made us work extremely hard in my previous job.
3  She never let me take any decisions.
4   Could you have Mr Clarke prepare some statistics?
5  She's finding it difficult to get used to the climate.
6  I feel it is necessary to delegate more of the work.

## Verb + *for* + *to*-infinitive

**A** Verb + *for* + *to*-infinitive

1  c    2  e    3  b    4  a    5  d

**B** Special cases

1  using    2  seeing    3  to inform    4  to tell    5  to work; having

## Unit 7

## Passives (1)

**A** Passive verb forms

**1** f　**2** d　**3** e　**4** a　**5** b　**6** c

**B** Focusing on the action

**1** *Das Kapital* was written by Karl Marx.

**2** Your car is being repaired now.

**3** Apple Computers was founded by Steve Jobs.

**4** The proposal will be discussed by the board.

**5** Was Mrs Wilson informed?

**6** Renault cars are made in Slovenia.

**7** He has been transferred to the New York office.

**8** The new conference centre was opened by the princess.

**9** A full investigation had been made.

**10** I didn't realise my telephone conversations were being listened to.

**C** Focusing on information

**1** should be read through

**2** absorbed

**3** a written document needs to be filed

**4** can be written on the document

**5** a note should be made

**6** All messages should be disposed of once they have been dealt with.

## Passives (2)

**A** Check your understanding

**1** false　**2** true　**3** true　**4** false　**5** true

**B** Active or passive?

**1** are tailored　**2** are given　**3** are conducted　**4** (are) designed　**5** encourage　**6** build
**7** show　**8** be saved　**9** be used　**10** be created　**11** help

**C** Describing a process

**1** are transported　**2** is removed　**3** is burnt　**4** be generated　**5** are cut　**6** cooked
**7** is bleached　**8** remove　**9** improve　**10** requires　**11** are mixed　**12** diluted
**13** is sprayed　**14** is pressed　**15** dried　**16** wound　**17** weighs　**18** is controlled
**19** correct

## Unit 8

### Ability

**A** Abilities

**1** b  **2** f  **3** e  **4** a  **5** g  **6** c  **7** d

**B** Past abilities

**1** managed to  **2** could  **3** managed to  **4** could  **5** managed to  **6** could  **7** could

**C** Indicating disapproval

**1** She could have contacted me on my mobile.  **3** We could have walked.

**2** She could have let me know.  **4** He could have sent me an e-mail.

### Obligation, prohibition

**A** Rules and regulations

*Specimen answers*

**1** You must not carry a gun.

**2** You have to pay to use buses and trams.

**3** You don't have to vote if you are over 18.

**4** You must not drink alcohol at work.

**5** You have to pay to drive on a motorway.

**6** You have to declare income earned abroad.

**7** You have to wear a seat belt when driving a car.

**B** Rules at work

**1** You must not take home company equipment.

**2** You don't have to wear a badge.

**3** You have to wear a tie, if you are a man.

**4** You must not wear jeans at work.

**5** You don't have to clock in when you arrive.

**6** You have to wear a dress or a suit, if you are a woman.

**C** Signs and notices

**1** You have to give way. / You must give way.

**2** You must not turn left.

**3** You must not overtake.

**4** You don't have to change your money into local currency.

**5** You must not drive over 30 mph. / You have to drive under 30 mph.

**6** You have to be a member to enter.

**7** You have to wear protective clothing. / You must not enter.

## Possibility

### A *can*

*Specimen answers*

1 Learning a foreign language can often be painful.
2 Entertaining overseas customers can sometimes be hard work.
3 Being in charge of a new project can often be challenging.
4 Setting up in business can occasionally be good fun.
5 Negotiating a contract can sometimes be a waste of time.

### B *could / couldn't*

1 If we diversified we could offer a wider range of products.
2 If I had stayed in the States I could have got a better job.
3 In the 1980s you could make a fortune as a 'golden boy'.
4 She could have done an MBA but decided it was too much work.
5 Thirty years ago you could buy cigarettes in packets of five.
6 Before privatisation you couldn't buy shares in British Telecom.

### C Missed opportunities

*Specimen answers*

He could have become a rock star.
He could have done research at Florida Atlantic University.
He could have become a film star.
He could have sailed in the Admiral's Cup.

## Likelihood

### A Degrees of likelihood

1 e    2 b    3 f    4 a    5 d    6 c    7 h    8 g

### B Expressions of likelihood

| | | |
|---|---|---|
| may come sooner | are also likely to produce | are highly likely |
| there is a 67% chance | are not likely to change | will probably be located |

## Permission, suggestions, offers

### A Permission, suggestions or offers?

1 suggestion    2 request for permission    3 offer    4 request for permission
5 request for permission    6 suggestion    7 offer    8 suggestion    9 offer

### B Offers and suggestions

1 We must get together
2 Do you need any help
3 Shall I hold the door open
4 Would you like me
5 I'll give you

## Willingness, refusal, promises, threats, typical behaviour

**A** Uses of *will* and *would*

**1** P **2** TB **3** R **4** TB **5** P **6** T **7** W **8** R **9** TB **10** T **11** W **12** TB

**B** *will*, *won't* or *would*?

1 Accidents will happen.

2 I'll do my best.

3 He won't accept her authority.

4 If you don't pay, legal action will be taken.

5 A fanatic is someone who can't change his mind and won't change the subject.

6 If you will be rude how can you expect people to like you?

7 He would smoke a large cigar before making an important decision.

8 The product with the better-known brand name will sell better than the other.

## Unit 9

## Types of multi-word verbs

**A** With or without an object?

**1** – **2** c **3** b **4** e **5** a **6** – **7** – **8** – **9** – **10** d

**B** Separable or inseparable?

**1** A **2** A **3** U **4** A **5** A **6** A **7** A **8** U **9** U **10** A **11** U **12** U **13** A **14** A **15** A

## Understanding multi-word verbs (1)

**A** Multi-word verbs with *up*

**1** e **2** f **3** b **4** a **5** c **6** d

**B** Sentence completion

**1** face up to **2** follow up **3** work up **4** look up **5** pay up **6** play up

**C** Sentence completion

**1** save up **2** clear up **3** keep up **4** set up **5** hold ... up **6** think up

## Understanding multi-word verbs (2)

**A** Multi-word verbs with *down*

**1** break down **2** run down **3** bring down **4** note down **5** cut down **6** play down

**B** Multi-word verbs with *up*, *down* and *over*

**1** e **2** c **3** a **4** b **5** g **6** f **7** d

# Understanding multi-word verbs (3)

**A** Particles and their meaning

**1**

   **1** e   **2** a   **3** d   **4** c   **5** b

**2**

   **2** spark off = beginning      **5** look over = considering
   **3** wind up = completing       **6** note down = writing /recording
   **4** sum up = completing       **7** keep on = continuing

**B** Sentence rearrangement

   **1** We need to make up for lost time.

   **2** They want to back out of the agreement.

   **3** The firm ran up against strong competition.

   **4** After a long delay he got round to drafting a reply.

   **5** A number of people have put in for the chairman's job.

   **6** Roger thinks he's come up with an answer to our problems.

**C** A phone conversation

   **1** put … through   **2** hold on   **3** call back   **4** tied up   **5** get back
   **6** fix up   **7** read … back

## Unit 10

# Adverb position and uses (1)

**A** Sentence rearrangement

   **1** I am still waiting for confirmation.     **4** I will probably be able to get it cheaper.

   **2** I never wear jeans at work.       **5** I am always pleased to welcome visitors.

   **3** He speaks Greek very well.       **6** Her idea is completely absurd.

**B** Adverb position

Hi! Thanks for your last e-mail. I'm *very* sorry I haven't got back to you sooner but we've been *terribly* rushed in the office. We *always* seem to be so busy. It seems the launch has been *remarkably* successful, beyond our wildest dreams in fact. We are *obviously* delighted and we have *already* had a large order from a company in China. This is *absolutely* fabulous news. See you soon.

**C** Describing the rate of change

*Specimen answers*

Sales of cotton trousers have risen substantially / rapidly / sharply.

Sales of casual corduroy trousers have gone up to some extent / gradually / slowly.

Sales of jeans have risen slightly.

## Adverb position and uses (2)

**A** Commenting on the situation

**1** d **2** c **3** e **4** f **5** b **6** a

**B** Your situation

*Specimen answers*

**1** They sometimes arrive late.

**2** I usually work in my office.

**3** I get on with her very badly.

**4** I haven't seen her lately.

**5** Quite honestly, I think her performance is awful.

**C** Adverb position

Thank you for the e-mail you sent *yesterday*. I have *already* spoken to Eric but he says he is *still* waiting for confirmation from the board before we can go ahead with the proposed changes. *Quite frankly*, the delay is getting on my nerves but I hope to get started on the project *very soon*. As is *often* the case, we will *suddenly* receive confirmation at the last minute and have to work *flat out* for the next couple of months in order to get into production *fast*.

## Unit 11

## Noun formation

**A** Noun formation

| | | | |
|---|---|---|---|
| acceptance | protection | weakness | complexity |
| agreement | racism / racist | reliability | effectiveness |
| counterfeiting | reference | prosperity | awareness |
| entry / entrance | storage | socialism / society | creativity / creation |
| initiation | wastage | punctuality | |
| occurrence | wisdom | reality | |

**B** Activities

**1** f **2** c **3** a **4** e **5** b **6** d

**C** People

**1** receptionist **2** employee **3** lawyer **4** accountant **5** musician **6** electrician
**7** reporter / journalist **8** photographer **9** applicants / candidates

## Types of noun

**A** Countable or uncountable?

**1** U **2** C **3** C **4** U **5** C **6** U **7** C **8** U **9** C **10** U **11** U **12** C

**B** Matching countable and uncountable nouns

| Countable | Uncountable |
|-----------|-------------|
| cars | traffic |
| machines | equipment |
| policies | insurance |
| accidents | damage |
| jobs | employment |
| journey | travel |
| hints | advice |
| bulletins | news |
| laws | legislation |

## Plural nouns

**A** Nouns only occurring in the plural

**1** outskirts    **2** means    **3** valuables    **4** goods    **5** premises    **6** works    **7** Refreshments    **8** crossroads

**B** Making nouns plural

**1** bags    **2** people    **3** parties    **4** formulas / formulae    **5** potatoes    **6** shelves    **7** faxes    **8** knives    **9** criteria    **10** matches

**C** Singular or plural?

**1** is    **2** have    **3** are    **4** are    **5** is    **6** has / have

**D** Common mistakes

**1** The news *is* bad, I'm afraid.

**2** She knows a great many *people*.

**3** Stress at work is not a recent *phenomenon*.

**4** Our office is situated in pleasant *surroundings*.

**5** The *staff* are unhappy with the new arrangements.

## Two nouns together

**A** Famous places

| | |
|---|---|
| Berlin's Brandenburg Gate | London's Big Ben |
| Venice's canals | New York's skyscrapers |
| Madrid's Prado | Cairo's pyramids |

**B** Quantities

a lump of sugar    a can of beer    a jar of coffee    a bar of chocolate    a carton of milk    a grain of salt

**C** Noun + *of* + noun

**1** basket of currencies    **2** breach of contract    **3** rate of return    **4** conflict of interest    **5** letter of credit

## Compound nouns

**A** Noun combinations

**1** sales  **2** account  **3** market  **4** brand  **5** trade

**B** Choice of structures

**1** ✓  **2** ✗  **3** ✗  **4** ✓  **5** ✓  **6** ✗  **7** ✓  **8** ✗  **9** ✓  **10** ✗  **11** ✓  **12** ✓
**13** ✗  **14** ✓  **15** ✗  **16** ✗  **17** ✗  **18** ✓

**C** Compound nouns

**1** production  **2** figures  **3** sense  **4** loyalty  **5** revenue

## Nouns and prepositions

**A** Which preposition?

**1** in  **2** in  **3** of  **4** for  **5** on  **6** for  **7** to  **8** under

**B** Prepositional phrases

**1** beyond  **2** by  **3** in  **4** on  **5** at

## Unit 12

## Articles (*a / an*, *the* and zero article)

**A** *a / an, the* and zero article

**3** (Cambridge) Category 13
**4** (The job) Category 6
**5** (antique clocks) Category 12
**6** (an idea) Category 1
**7** (The CBI) Category 9
**8** (people) Category 12
**9** (a training course) Category 1
**10** (a loan) Category 1
**11** (a small business) Category 1
**12** (the school) Category 5
**13** (the children) Category 6
**14** (the unemployed) Category 8
**15** (information) Category 11
**16** (different sources) Category 12
**17** (advice) Category 11
**18** (an accountant) Category 2
**19** (the village) Category 5/6
**20** (the antique trade) Category 8
**21** (a month) Category 3
**22** (the best thing) Category 10

**B** Ferrari

**1** a  **2** Ø  **3** the  **4** the  **5** a  **6** The  **7** the  **8** a  **9** Ø  **10** Ø  **11** Ø
**12** the  **13** the  **14** Ø  **15** the  **16** the  **17** The  **18** a  **19** the  **20** the  **21** the

## Quantifiers (1)

### A Amounts

**1** any  **2** no  **3** some  **4** Some  **5** None  **6** some  **7** any  **8** no; any  **9** some
**10** any; none  **11** any  **12** Some

### B A letter of complaint

**1** none  **2** any  **3** no  **4** some  **5** all  **6** any  **7** no

## Quantifiers (2)

### A Correct the errors

**1** He didn't reply fast enough.

**2** The flood caused a lot of damage.

**3** What she said was a little strange.

**4** The whole process uses very little electricity.

**5** I enjoyed a few of her books, but not all of them.

**6** We haven't made much / a lot of progress recently.

**7** I don't think he has enough experience for the job.

**8** She works mostly on her own so she has very few colleagues.

**9** I've got a few minutes to spare so we can continue if you like.

**10** The final date for submission was three weeks ago so it's far too late now.

### B A memo

**1** a little  **2** few  **3** much  **4** little  **5** few  **6** many  **7** too / a little  **8** a great deal of
**9** a few  **10** enough

## Unit 13

## Adjectives

### A Your personal profile
Individual responses

### B Adjective formation

**1** successful  **2** scientific  **3** competitive  **4** responsible  **5** promotional  **6** autonomous
**7** accurate  **8** technical  **9** competent  **10** loyal

## Compound adjectives

### A Compound adjectives

**1** free  **2** self  **3** market  **4** well  **5** term  **6** anti

**B** Adjectives and nouns

foregone conclusion   joint account   last resort   heated exchange   stumbling block
high priority   stiff competition   vested interest

**1** stiff competition   **2** joint account   **3** heated exchange   **4** high priority   **5** last resort
**6** stumbling block   **7** foregone conclusion   **8** vested interest

## Adjective position

**A** Which adjective?

**1** former   **2** last   **3** previous   **4** present   **5** major   **6** obvious

**B** Before or after the noun?

**1** issues discussed   **2** money allocated   **3** points raised   **4** uniform issued
**5** goods ordered   **6** women questioned   **7** outstanding ability   **8** involved argument

**C** Sentence rearrangement

**1** The statement issued by the government was misinterpreted.

**2** The problems raised during the meeting have been solved.

**3** The main thing is that you shouldn't worry.

**4** Her refusal to cooperate has put me in an impossible situation.

## Adjectives and adverbs

**A** Common mistakes

**1** She likes driving fast cars. ✓

**2** I work hard because I am highly paid.

**3** She's a very friendly person. ✓

**4** Everything I do recently seems to go wrong.

**5** We need to start early.

**6** Dealing with the Y2K problem was a costly business. ✓

**7** Time is running short.

**B** Adverb position

**1** extremely   **2** increasingly   **3** unfortunately   **4** deeply   **5** awfully   **6** suitably
**7** easily   **8** hugely

## Prepositions of place and direction

**A** Which preposition?

**1** in   **2** across   **3** (a)round   **4** at / by   **5** through   **6** beyond   **7** from   **8** to

**B** Sentence completion

**1** around / about   **2** from   **3** in   **4** on   **5** from; (a)round   **6** through; from; to   **7** by
**8** in; to   **9** down / up / across   **10** beyond

## Prepositions of time

**A** Which preposition?

**1** on   **2** in   **3** through   **4** at; on   **5** in   **6** from; to   **7** in   **8** beyond
**9** by   **10** around

**B** Prepositions of time

*Specimen answers*

He's leaving tomorrow on flight BA 515 to Paris and staying at the Hotel du Nord.
On 4 May he's meeting Monsieur Vatel at 22 rue Danton.
He's coming back from France at 4.45pm on 5 May.
The following day there's a board meeting from 10 o'clock to 12.30.
The phone bill must be paid by 7 May.
Jane's coming back from Dublin around 11.30 on 8 May.
On 9 May he has to pick Lucy up from her dance lesson at 5pm.
On 10 May the new share option scheme comes into force.
On 11 May there'll be a dinner party from 8pm until midnight.

## Unit 14

## Advising

**A** Giving advice

**1** If you don't hurry up you'll miss the plane.

**2** My advice would be to sell your shares now.

**3** Don't drive through the city centre during rush hour.

**4** You'd better see a doctor if you're feeling ill.

**5** You'd better not tell her the bad news yet.

**6** If I were you, I'd declare my overseas investments to the tax authorities.

**7** It's worth asking for a second opinion.

**B** If I were you …

*Specimen answer*

My advice would be to keep Mr Mudd in Customer Relations as he is unlikely to be of much use elsewhere. In my opinion, his salary should now be frozen unless he agrees to take on more responsibility and justify his higher salary.

## Agreeing and disagreeing

**A** *so / neither*

**1** Neither did I.    **3** So should I.    **5** So do I.
**2** Neither can I.    **4** Neither have I.    **6** So do I.

**B** Shades of opinion

*Specimen answers*

1 All men and women should do military service.

I disagree with that completely.

2 There should be a single world currency.

Yes, but you still have to remember that people are attached to their currencies.

3 National industries should be protected.

Yes, I'd go along with that up to a point but you can't ignore market forces entirely.

4 Smoking at work should be banned.

That's out of the question.

5 Men and women should retire at 55.

You may have a point but what about the social security deficit?

## Asking for information

**A** Asking questions

2 *Are* you single or married?

3 *Where* do you live?

4 *How old* are you?

5 *What* do you do for a living?

6 *How long* have you been working for your present employer?

7 *How much* do you earn?

8 *How often* do you go abroad?

9 *When* did you last have to make a presentation in English?

10 *Why* do you need training in foreign languages?

11 *Which* of these words describes your ability in English: beginner, intermediate or advanced?

**B** A bad line

1 How many people visited the plant?

2 Who congratulated me?

3 Who complimented me? (*or* Which director complimented me?)

## Comparing products and services

**A** Making comparisons

1 b    2 d    3 f    4 a    5 g    6 h    7 e    8 c

**B** Common mistakes

1 Lisbon is not as big *as* London.

2 There is more to life *than* a spreadsheet.

3 The advantage of this project is that it is *twice as cheap as* the other.

**4** Women's pay used to be *much* lower than men's, even for *the* same work.

**5** Metro is the world's second *biggest* retailer after Wal-Mart Stores of the US.

**C  The top headhunting firms**

**1** the largest    **2** most strongly    **3** even closer    **4** a little less    **5** much more

## Complaining and apologising

**A  A letter of complaint**

**1** I will have no alternative but to

**2** I am writing to express my concern

**3** Regrettably,

The order of the letter is as follows:
Dear Mrs O'Malley,
I am writing to express my concern ...
Regrettably, this delay ...
Given the long-standing relationship ...
However, if the delay continues ...
I look forward to ...
Yours sincerely,

**B  A letter of apology**

**1** We are very concerned

**2** We very much regret

**3** I assure you we are doing everything in our power

**4** Once again, we apologise

**5** hope you will understand the reason

## Confirming information

**A  Confirming decisions**

**1** wasn't she    **2** didn't she    **3** didn't he    **4** did he    **5** would it    **6** didn't we
**7** shouldn't we    **8** isn't it    **9** hadn't we    **10** shall we

**B  A conversation at a cocktail party**

**1** aren't you?    **2** weren't you?    **3** isn't it?    **4** haven't you?    **5** shall I?

## Describing a company

**A  HMV**

**1** comprises    **2** the world's foremost    **3** leading    **4** operates    **5** worldwide

**B** Wieden & Kennedy

**1** world-class **2** headquartered **3** operations **4** range **5** headquarters
**6** located **7** employs

**C** Sita

*Specimen answer*

Based in Geneva, SITA is a major player in the field of telecommunications and ranks No. 1 for the number of connections worldwide. We are present in 225 countries with over 900 separate locations generating a revenue of $1 billion and employing more than 5,000 people.

## Describing processes

**A** Active or passive?

**1** integrates **2** relies **3** is coordinated **4** ensures **5** is managed **6** be synthesised
**7** be scheduled **8** is given **9** are checked **10** be used **11** been met
**12** be warehoused **13** been fulfilled **14** are given **15** is built up **16** be located
**17** be limited

## Describing trends

**A** Trends in consumer relationships

**1** has changed (the change is described as complete)

**2** have never seen

**3** has replaced

**4** have never had

**5** have realised / have been realising (the change is still under way, although some companies may have become fully aware of the change)

**6** has been based

**7** have been re-examining

**8** have taken / have been taking

**9** has become

**B** Describing trends

*Specimen answers*

During the 1990s the annual percentage change in GDP rose steadily in Western Germany despite a 2% drop from 1994–95. Since then growth has been steady.

In contrast, there was a sharp decrease in 1994 in Eastern Germany. In 1995 there was a marked recovery, but since then growth has been erratic.

From 1996–2000 the number of Internet users in Japan increased steadily, even though until 1997 the number of users as a percentage of the population fell. But since then the numbers have continued to go up and are still rising.

# Forecasting and speculating

## A Forecasting

*Specimen answers*

1 I'm likely to get a pay rise soon.

2 My firm is unlikely to be taken over.

3 I'm very unlikely to be made redundant.

4 I'm bound to get promoted.

5 There is bound to be a change of government in the next six months

## B Speculating

**1b** She looks so young; she *can't* be a day over 30.

**2a** She can speak English and Spanish perfectly; she *must* come from a bilingual family.

**3e** She *can't* know what's in the report; she hasn't had a copy.

**4f** She *must* have friends in high places because she's survived three major scandals.

**5d** She *must* know Berlin pretty well; she lived there for three years.

**6c** She *can't* have much of a social life; she works 60 hours a week.

## C Making hypotheses

*Specimen answers*

1 The director must have had inside knowledge.

2 The employees must have got food poisoning.

3 He can't have spoken to her in Urdu.

4 He must have been embezzling the money.

# Getting things done

## A Getting things done

1 We get / have all our export risks insured.

2 I have my car serviced by the garage every 15,000 kilometres.

3 We get a specialist agency to translate all the company documentation and manuals.

   We get / have all the company documentation and manuals translated by a specialist agency.

4 We're having a new extension built by the contractors.

   We're having the contractors build a new extension.

5 I had the contract drawn up by the legal department.

   I had the legal department draw up the contract.

## B Arranging for things to be done

1 We need to get / have the printer fixed.

2 We'll need to get / have her replaced.

3 I need to get / have them cleaned.

4 I need to have them checked.

## Giving instructions

### A Changing a wheel

1 Park the car on a flat, stable surface and apply the handbrake firmly.  (C)
2 Raise the vehicle off the ground with a jack.  (G)
3 Prise out the centre hub cap.  (A)
4 Unscrew the wheel bolts.  (E)
5 Remove the wheel and replace it with the spare.  (F)
6 Tighten the wheel bolts.  (H)
7 Replace the centre hub cap.  (D)
8 Lower the vehicle and remove the jack.  (B)

### B Giving directions

## Planning ahead

*Specimen answers*

1 Who is going to print the programme? How many copies will you be needing?
2 How will the delegates be getting from the airport to the hotel?
3 What are they going to do in the evening? / What kind of entertainment are you planning to put on?
4 Who will be making the opening address?
5 What are you planning for / to do after dinner on Tuesday evening?
6 Which room will you be holding the plenary session in?
7 What will Rod Weir be talking about?
8 What do you intend to provide for vegetarians?
9 How many rooms will you be needing for the workshops?
10 What size rooms are you going to use?
11 What equipment will you be needing?
12 What time will they be going back to the airport?

# Reporting what people say or think (1)

**A** Reporting what the MD said

1 He said (that) he thought a joint venture was the best way to break into the Middle East.

2 He said (that) he was / we were not planning to set up a subsidiary.

3 He said (that) he had been talking to a group of investors in the Gulf.

4 He said (that) he'd talked to the commercial attaché at the embassy.

5 He said (that) he didn't want to diversify in the immediate future.

6 He said (that) we shouldn't attempt to move too fast because we might get our fingers burned.

7 He said (that) he / we would be sending Stuart Campbell on a fact-finding mission.

**B** News in brief

1 e   2 c   3 a   4 b   5 d

# Reporting what people say or think (2)

**A** The minutes of a meeting

1 raised   2 invited   3 outlined   4 acknowledged   5 reminded   6 pointed out
7 disagreed   8 advised   9 complained   10 confirmed   11 suggested   12 offered
13 warned

# Reporting questions

**A** Sentence transformation

2 She asked me if I had seen Bernard yet.

3 Could you tell me if you are open on a Saturday?

4 He wondered if / whether I had got his message.

5 Have you any idea how much time there is left?

6 She wanted to know if / whether she would be taking her husband with her.

**B** Enquiries

2 Someone asked her where you can get a shuttle (from).

3 Someone asked her where you can get foreign currency.

4 Someone asked her where the duty free was.

5 Someone asked her where they could leave their suitcases.

6 Someone asked her why the Alitalia flight had been delayed.

# Requesting and offering

**A** Polite requests

*Specimen answers*

1 Do you mind if I leave early?

I'm sorry, you can't.

**2** Shall I give you a lift?

That's very kind of you.

**3** I was wondering if you could lend me $50 until tomorrow.

Well, I'm afraid I haven't got any money.

**4** Would you like a glass of sherry?

No, thanks. I don't drink sherry.

**5** Could I have the bill, please?

Certainly.

**6** Could you tell me the way to the station, please?

I'm afraid I don't know where it is.

**B Doing someone a favour**

**1** I'm afraid   **2** Shall I   **3** go ahead   **4** I was wondering if   **5** I'll   **6** could you possibly

**A** Could I ask you a favour?

**B** Yeah, go ahead.

**A** I was wondering if you could phone these people in Spain for me. My Spanish is atrocious.

**B** No problem. Just tell me what you want me to say.

**A** Shall I write it down for you?

**B** Yes. Otherwise I'll forget! When do you want me to phone them?

**A** Tomorrow.

**B** Well, I'm afraid I can't tomorrow. I'm not coming in to the office.

**A** Well, could you possibly do it the day after tomorrow?

**B** Sure. I'll do it first thing.

## Suggesting

**A Making suggestions**

**1 b** How about hiring a new public relations manager?

**2 e** How about offering her some kind of promotion to a more highly-paid position?

**3 a** Shall we stay in a nearby hotel overnight?

**4 c** Well, I suggest taking them to a night club.

**5 d** We could give people more responsibility for decision-making.

**B Problem-solving**

*Specimen answers*

**1** I suggest that we should review our internal promotion policy.

**2** Why don't we use a factoring agency?

**3** Shouldn't we offer a bigger discount?

**4** You could sell them at reduced prices to the employees and their families.

**5** I think you should do what you can reasonably do in worktime and leave the rest.

## Understanding signs and notices

### Signs and notices

**1** c    **2** a    **3** b    **4** i    **5** d    **6** c    **7** g    **8** f    **9** e    **10** h    **11** g    **12** b    **13** a

## Unit 15

## Adding and combining information

**A** Definitions: a financial quiz

**1e  The over-the-counter market** is the market *where* securities are traded outside a regular exchange.

**2d  Options** are financial instruments *that/which* give the right but not the obligation to buy or sell a commodity at a certain price.

**3f  Floating exchange rates** are the values of currencies *whose* fluctuations against each other are set by market forces.

**4b  Bears** are investors *who* believe share prices are likely to fall.

**5g  A preference share** is a share *that/which* guarantees holders a prior claim on dividends.

**6c  Names** are wealthy individuals *who* provide funds to back Lloyd's insurance policies.

**7a  A stock exchange** is a market *where* shares and government bonds are bought and sold.

**B** *Whose, who, which, that*

**1** whose    **2** who    **3** which    **4** whose    **5** that / which    **6** that / which

## Emphasising

**A** Ajaz Ahmed

**1** truly    **2** to say the least    **3** whole    **4** whatsoever    **5** total    **6** Indeed    **7** so    **8** such

## Expressing a reaction

**A** Indicating attitude

**1** understandably    **2** Paradoxically    **3** typically    **4** mysteriously    **5** conveniently

**B** Exclamations

| | |
|---|---|
| **1** How extravagant! | **1** What a mess! |
| **2** What a mess! | **2** How extravagant! |
| **3** What rubbish! | **3** How disgusting! |
| **4** How awful! | **4** How lucky! |
| **5** What a fantastic idea! | **5** What rubbish! |
| **6** How disgusting! | **6** How awful! |
| **7** How lucky! | **7** What a fantastic idea! |

## Generalising / indicating relevance

**A** General statements

  **1** by and large  **2** All in all  **3** On the whole  **4** As a rule  **5** In general

**B** *... speaking*

  **1** Aesthetically speaking  **2** Broadly speaking  **3** Technically speaking  **4** relatively speaking

**C** Points of view

  **1** From a military point of view, it is better to use aircraft to bomb strategic targets before using ground troops.

  **2** From an ethical point of view, it is wrong to do to other people what you would not want done to you.

  **3** From an environmental point of view, it is better to build on 'brownfield' rather than 'greenfield' sites.

  **4** From a scientific point of view, Jupiter is an extremely interesting planet.

  **5** From a financial point of view, it doesn't make sense to buy stocks when they've reached their peak.

## Highlighting information

**A** Highlighting information

  **1** f  **2** b  **3** a  **4** d  **5** e  **6** c

**B** Focusing on the topic

  **1**

    **1** What we need is a good overseas partner.

    **2** What you have to have is the right distribution network.

    **3** What you must do is make sure your products are suited to the local market.

  **2**

    **1** What I will do first is give you an idea of how the project started.

    **2** What I will do then is describe the project in more detail.

    **3** What I want to do is convince you that this project is worth investing in.

**C** Negative ideas

  **1** Never will we allow our firm to be taken over.

  **2** Under no circumstances should you handle dangerous products without protective clothing.

  **3** On no account must you tell him about our plans.

## Linking (1)

**A** Contrasting

  **1** Despite  **2** Although  **3** Yet  **4** Although  **5** Nevertheless  **6** Whereas

**B** Link words

  **1** Although  **2** However  **3** Despite  **4** whereas

# Linking (2)

**A** Categories of link words

| Contrast | Result | Extra information | Sequencing in time |
|---|---|---|---|
| on the other hand | so | furthermore | meanwhile |
| even so | therefore | moreover | subsequently |
| nevertheless | thus | also | eventually |
| alternatively | consequently | too | formerly |

**B** Link the statements

**1** b  **2** e  **3** a  **4** c  **5** f  **6** d

# Substituting

**A** *so* and *not*

**1** Yes, I expect so.  **3** Yes, I guess so.  **5** No, I hope not.

**2** Yes, I imagine so.  **4** No, I'm afraid not.  **6** No, I suppose not.

**B** Avoiding repetition

**1** I may be free this afternoon. If so, I'll come and see you.

**2** Africa has long had a bad reputation for business – companies investing there fear the unknown, and often rightly so.

**3** A senior monetary official said that he regretted the decision not to join the EMU in 1999 for one particular reason: the operational structure of the Bank of England would have made a perfect role model for the European Central Bank – much more so than the German Bundesbank.

**C** Referring

This new authority = an International Credit Insurance Corporation

This = the obligation to provide data on all borrowings

those amounts = the amounts it is willing to insure

these = the amounts it is willing to insure

This = the basis of its judgement

This = the capital consisting of SDRs

those countries = the borrowing countries

such an institution = the International Credit Insurance Corporation

such a period = a time when international lending is in a state of collapse

## Unit 16

## Managing a conversation (1)

**A** Introducing a topic

*Specimen answers*

1 Have you heard that Christine is leaving?
2 Did you go to the performance of *The Magic Flute*?
3 Have you heard about the latest developments?
4 Did you hear about the disaster in the planning department?

**B** Changing a topic

*Specimen answers*

1 By the way, did he arrange for overtime at the weekend?
2 While we're on the subject of China, did you hear what happened in Beijing?
3 This is on a completely different subject, but Sandra wants to move into another section.

**C** Echoing

**A** And if you book before the end of the month you get a 10% reduction.
**B** Before the end of the month?
**A** Yeah, that's what it said on the leaflet.

**C** Well, I thought there was something wrong with the system.
**D** Something wrong?
**C** Yeah, but it was working all right in the morning.

## Managing a conversation (2)

**A** *sort of / kind of*

1 c   2 c   3 a   4 c   5 b

**B** Conversational acts

1 d   2 a   3 e   4 b   5 c

## Negotiating

**A** Negotiating an agreement

1 d   2 b   3 c   4 a

## Presenting figures

**A** Saying figures aloud

1 oh/zero point four five

**2** one point eight five

**3** seven hundred fifty-nine dollars (US) / seven hundred and fifty-nine dollars (UK)

**4** a/one hundred and twenty-five million yen

**5** a third / one-third

**6** two-fifths

**7** one in three; a ratio of one to three

**8** two thousand and one

**9** three four two five four six one

**10** three seven four nine

**B In your situation?**

*Specimen answers*

**1** About 10% of my time is spent in leisure activities.

**2** On average, 2.2 children are born to each couple.

**3** It's in the region of the equivalent of £25,000 a year.

**4** It's 4.75%.

**5** It's about 3%.

**6** One in three employees is a woman.

# Presenting information

**A Presenting a company**

**1** I'd like first of all to give you an overview

**2** Firstly

**3** secondly

**4** thirdly

**5** As you can see from the transparency

**6** And to complete the picture

**7** Now I would like to describe

**8** If you look at

**9** Then

**10** So to recapitulate

# Presenting visual information

**A Illustrations**

**1** flow chart   **2** graph   **3** pie chart   **4** bar chart   **5** table   **6** diagram   **7** vertical axis
**8** horizontal axis   **9** curve   **6** dotted line

**B Describing graphs**

**1 1** at   **2** from   **3** of   **4** under   **5** of   **6** by   **7** to

**2** Real GDP growth in Japan rose by 3% between 1994 and 1995 but slumped over the next three years. It picked up again between 1998 and 1999 and grew slowly after that.

The yen declined against the dollar between 1994 and 1999 but then recovered slowly.

As a percentage of GDP, Japan's budget deficit dipped by 2% between 1994 and mid-1995, but rose substantially in the next year. However, since then it has plummeted to a deficit representing 10% of GDP.

## Social interaction

**A** Reacting to what people say

**1** You're joking!   **2** I didn't quite catch that.   **3** How come?   **4** Never mind.   **5** Oh dear!

**a** How come?   **b** Never mind.   **c** You're joking!   **d** Oh dear!   **e** I didn't quite catch that.

**B** Conversational pairs

**1** i   **2** g   **3** h   **4** b   **5** f   **6** a   **7** j   **8** c   **9** d   **10** e

## Taking part in meetings

**A** Chairing a meeting

**1** d   **2** g   **3** h   **4** a   **5** f   **6** e   **7** c   **8** b

**B** Taking part in a meeting

**1** f   **2** e   **3** a   **4** c   **5** d   **6** b

## Telephoning

**A** A phone conversation

**2** Hello. My name's Beata Szlachetka. I'd like to speak to Katie Chapman, please.

**3** Sorry, I didn't quite catch that.

**4** Beata Szlachetka and I'd like to speak to Katie Chapman.

**5** Hold the line, please. I'll see if she's in.

**6** (pause) Hello. Katie Chapman speaking.

**7** Hello, this is Beata.

**8** Hi, Beata. How are you doing?

**9** Fine, thanks. And you?

**10** OK. Busy as usual.

**11** I'm just ringing to find out if you've received the copies of the contract.

**12** Yeah, they came this morning but I haven't signed them yet.

**13** OK, there's no rush.

**14** I'll sign them this afternoon and send them back to you.

**15** Great. Thanks a lot.

**B** Telephone language

Numbers 7 and 8 are recorded messages.

**C** Taking someone's name

Graham Hughes

Janice Young

# Index

The first number refers to page number in the book. The second number refers to the number of the entry on that page. For example:

**articles** 88 means that you can read about articles on page 88.

**going to** 24,2; 24,3; 126,2 means you can read about the uses of *going to* on page 24 (sections 2 and 3) and on page 126 (section 2).